ADVANCED DRIVING
THE ESSENTIAL GUIDE

© 2007 the IAM.
Skill For Life is
facilitated by the IAM.
Published in
conjunction with MBI
Publishing Company,
St. Paul, MN, USA

FIRST EDITION
All rights reserved. No part of this publication
may be reproduced or transmitted in any form or
by any means, electronic or mechanical, including
photocopying, recording or in any information
storage retrieval system, without the prior
written permission of the IAM.

Words & photos by John Sootheran
Designed by Mark Guest
Reprographics by AT Graphics
Printed in China
ISBN 978-0-7603-3314-3
This book was created with the invaluable input
of Stephen Mead and Anthony Swing

ADVANCED DRIVING
THE ESSENTIAL GUIDE

Experience the pleasure of driving safely and progressively

HOW TO USE THIS BOOK

This book should be used for self-study and to supplement
expert advice from the Institute of Advanced Motorists' representatives in
preparation for taking the Advanced Driving Challenge.
The way it is organised allows you to find the relevant subjects and
advice quickly and easily under general headings.
The most important aspects of Advanced Driving are summarised at the
end of each of the major topics, under the headings:
Advanced checklist – *What you should be achieving.*
Examiner checklist – *What the examiner is looking for you to achieve.*

MOTORBOOKS

"Both my sons are now Advanced Drivers too. What better way to protect the most important people in your life?"

Foreword by Nigel Mansell

As someone who is passionate about driving, I've always strived to be as good as I can be behind the wheel. While this allowed me to earn my living on the world's racetracks, I know that driving skill is just as important on the road.

This book gives you all the information and advice you'll need to become an Advanced Driver; it will help you take your driving to the next level.

On Britain's crowded highways, excellent vision, awareness, anticipation and car control are essential, and I believe there is no better way to hone these skills than by taking the IAM's *Skill For Life* Advanced Driving challenge.

I'm not sure whether I was more nervous on the grid of my first Grand Prix in 1980, or during my own IAM Test. What I do know is that I found achieving both goals extremely satisfying – as I'm sure did fellow racers: Graham Hill, Sir Stirling Moss, John Surtees and Geoff Duke – all IAM Advanced Drivers.

I was so impressed with the IAM scheme that both of my sons are now Advanced Drivers too. What better way to protect the most important people in your life?

With this in mind, I urge you to play your part, and make Britain's roads a better place to drive.

Becoming an Advanced Driver is an enjoyable and challenging experience from 'starting grid' to 'chequered flag'. I wish you good luck.

Nigel Mansell OBE
IAM President
Formula 1 World Champion 1992
American CART Champion 1993

"Advanced Driving isn't about pootling along annoying other road users... it's about making excellent progress, safely and courteously."

A testimonial from the author

Like many people, I'd always assumed that Advanced Driving was for doddery old folk in string-back driving gloves, who take a strange delight in self-righteously holding up speeding traffic in the fast lane of the motorway.

Then, three years ago, I decided to take the Advanced Driving challenge, to see once and for all if I was 'above-average' behind the wheel.

On a bright spring day in 2004, the A605 to Wellingborough became my 'road to Damascus'. In five brief minutes as a passenger to my Advanced Instructor, it became blindingly obvious that there was much more to this driving malarkey than I'd ever dreamt possible, and that the standard DOT driving test had only trained me to exploit, at best, about 40 percent of my driving ability.

On those twisty roads through Northants and Bedfordshire, I quickly learnt that advanced driving isn't about pootling along at 30mph annoying other road users. Quite the opposite in fact – it's about making excellent progress, safely and courteously.

Fast-forward 12 months, and I find myself driving through central Wales at 7am on a bright, dry day. The smooth, snaking roads and my Honda Civic Type R are soul mates and by applying my Advanced Driver training I have the most stupendous, exhilarating and truly memorable drive of my life... without once breaking the speed limit or taking a risk.

If, like me, you feel that driving is about more than just getting from A to B, then I absolutely guarantee that passing the *Skill For Life* challenge and becoming an Advanced Driver will enhance your motoring enjoyment, inspire confidence in those around you... oh, and save you a few quid on your insurance.

John Sootheran
IAM Advanced Driver since Spring 2004

THE ESSENTIAL GUIDE TO ADVANCED DRIVING
CONTENTS

"If you feel that driving is about more than just getting from A to B, passing the *Skill For Life* challenge will enhance your driving enjoyment. Guaranteed."

www.iam.org.uk

What Advanced Driving is about

- Being in total control... all the time.
- Brilliant observation and timing at junctions and roundabouts, so that you can negotiate the traffic with minimal disruption.
- Progressive driving where conditions allow.
- Effective overtaking.
- Awareness of other road users' behaviour.
- Understanding how your car works, and getting the most out of it.

GO ON, GET INVOLVED

By reading this book and showing an interest in Advanced Driving, you're already well on the way to improving your driving skills. Completing the course, makes you 70% less likely to be involved in an accident than an ordinary driver.

Advanced Driving isn't for everyone, but by studying this book and applying some of what you learn, you WILL become a more complete driver.

Advanced Drivers do... drive with excellent precision and awareness. They anticipate the danger created by other drivers' mistakes, and they allow a big enough safety margin to avoid getting into trouble themselves. That makes them confident, decisive drivers, always keen to make good progress.

Advanced Drivers don't... drive too slowly, always worrying what danger might be around the next bend. They never 'lose their cool' behind the wheel, and always try to accommodate other drivers' mistakes.

Commit some time and energy to *Skill For Life* and you'll soon take your driving to another level.

HOW YOU'LL BENEFIT FROM TAKING THE ADVANCED DRIVING CHALLENGE

• You get the satisfaction and confidence of knowing you're a safe, competent and courteous driver.
• You're part of an ever-growing number of Advanced Drivers.
• You're 70% less likely to crash your car than an ordinary driver.
• Many insurance companies give substantial discounts to Advanced Drivers, so your fees could easily be repaid in the first years after you pass.
• You get all the benefits of being an IAM member and a skill for life.

HOW TO BECOME AN IAM ADVANCED DRIVER

This book contains all the information you need to become a safe driver – an IAM Advanced Driver.

Combine the contents of this book with a little commitment, and expert help from the IAM's fleet trainers or volunteer observers, and you could be experiencing all the benefits of being a qualified Advanced Driver in a matter of months.

Read this book, learn and practise all the key points, then sign up for the *Skill For Life* driving course.

SIGNING UP TO *SKILL FOR LIFE*

Skill For Life **can be taken in two ways:**
• The standard *Skill For Life* course is run by the IAM's volunteer force of expert observers. You take as long as you need to prepare for the challenge – a typical driver takes eight sessions to prepare for the 90-minute test.
• *Skill For Life* can be completed more quickly through IAM Fleet Training with the help of a professional trainer. This involves intensive sessions over one day or two half-days, with one trainee to one professional coach, followed, once you're ready, by the 90-minute test. At the conclusion of your formal training or observed drives, your test application will be submitted by your trainer or observer. You will then be contacted by an examiner in your area to arrange the test.

Taking the IAM Advai

• You'll meet up with the examiner at an agreed location. There are over 300 IAM routes around the UK.

• You take the challenge in your own car, which must be road legal.

• A valid driving licence, car insurance policy and MOT certificate (if required) must be presented before the test can begin.

• The challenge takes about 90 minutes and covers 35 to 40 miles.

• The route will incorporate all types of roads and conditions. Motorways (where possible), dual-carriageways, country roads and urban streets.

• You should drive the way you have been shown by your fleet trainer or volunteer observer.

• You must always stick to the speed limits, whilst driving as progressively as conditions allow.

• You may be asked to reverse into a specific position, manoeuvre into a parking space or generally demonstrate your manoeuvring and reversing skills.

• The examiner will give you directions and make spot checks on your powers of observation.

• At the end, the examiner – who holds one of the highest levels of driving qualifications in the world – will tell you whether you will be recommended for membership. If you are not recommended you can retake the challenge at a later date.

• The challenge is presented in a friendly, non-intimidating way.

• A few minor faults don't preclude you from becoming an IAM member, but infringements of the law will not be condoned.

• You cannot take the Advanced Driving challenge if you currently have seven points or more on your licence. However, you would still be able to undergo Advanced Driver preparation, ready to take the challenge when your points are reduced.

:ed Driving Challenge

OTHER ADVANCED DRIVING OPTIONS

DriveCheck
DriveCheck assesses your driving skills – highlighting, and allowing you to eliminate, any bad driving habits you may have developed.

It is not a driving test, just an opportunity to keep your driving skills in tip-top condition.

DriveCheck participants become associate members of the IAM, so they can go on to do the *Skill For Life* challenge at a reduced rate.

Older Driver Assessment
Your reaction times and the quality of your vision can deteriorate with age. The IAM recognises this and offers an *Older Driver Assessment* which gives you in-depth feedback on your driving, helping you to stay at the top of your driving game.

Phone 0208 996 9600 or log on to www.iam.org.uk for further details of all driver training and assessment.

It's a jungle out

Each time you take to the streets in your car, you're facing a
Check out this picture. It highlights the sort of risks you could

The Fiddler
21% Eating fast food on his knee
24% On the phone
5% Fiddling with Sat Nav
13% Changing CD
21% Getting cigarettes out of jacket (on back seat!)
16% Admiring reflection

The Unfit Driver
26% Poor eyesight
17% No test taken
9% The shakes
36% Panicking
12% Drowsy on medication

The Pressured Sales Rep
41% Late for an appointment
11% Been up since 5am
9% Bad day
13% On the phone
6% Road-rage
20% Thinking about tomorrow's presentation

there!

whole host of potential dangers.
ace in your everyday driving

The New Driver
8% First time driving alone
42% Never been in this
much traffic
15% What does that sign
mean?
22% Which lane?
13% Sheer panic

Unlicenced Driver
14% No driver training
7% No licence
54% No insurance
9% No car maintenance
16% Bad attitude

School-Run Mum
28% Doing make-up
11% Brushing hair
27% Whining kids
9% Late for school
7% Shoes in footwell
18% Exhausted

OTHER HAZARDS
- diesel spillage
- car with broken brake lights
- car with poor brakes/tyres
- poor road surface
- worn road markings
- low, blinding sunlight
- hidden sign posts

These are just a few of the hazards you'll discover on
Britain's roads. The IAM's *Skill For Life* challenge prepares
you to deal with all of them.

The standard driving test

The Government has made the standard Driving Test more difficult in recent years, with the addition of a multiple-choice written test and a computerised hazard-awareness assessment. However it still only involves learning the most fundamental driving skills and doesn't include preparation for poor-weather or motorway driving.

The standard L-test is simply an introduction to driving a vehicle. Your 'further education' takes place on today's congested roads and provides a steep and often precarious learning curve. This is where IAM Advanced Driver education comes in. The more in-depth and rounded content of *Skill For Life* coaching will prepare

you for virtually any situation you're likely to encounter – and give you the observation skills and anticipation to avoid many incidents and hazards you were previously unaware of!

In essence, you can condense a lifetime's driving experience into a few months, with the IAM *Skill For Life* challenge. That said, even Advanced Drivers continue to learn and hone their skills every time they get into a car.

Banishing all those bad habits you've developed since passing your test is another great reason to become an Advanced Driver. Simply applying what you learn in this book will make every car journey safer, smoother, and often, quicker and more enjoyable.

"The standard L-test only involves learning the most fundamental driving skills."

YOUR VEHICLE

Spend just 10 minutes a week checking your car's fluid levels, tyre pressures, tread depth, light bulbs and windscreen wipers.

Clean your windows, lights, number-plates and mirrors regularly too. You'll not only be a lot safer, you'll also get the best performance, economy and reliability from your car.

YOUR STATE OF MIND

On the UK's congested roads it's important that you're always in the right frame of mind to drive.

Positive attitudes will help to reduce the risk of collisions through tolerance and courtesy, by being realistic as to your own abilities, and by maintaining a high degree of care for your own safety and that of others.

Driving on UK roads can be very stressful, but Advanced Drivers always remain cool-headed, tolerant and courteous – helping to avoid or diffuse any threatening situations.

Don't let your driving standards be affected by other motorist's mistakes or behaviour. Stay relaxed, don't be provoked and remember that, if you do make a mistake, an apologetic wave is often all it takes to put things right.

Advanced Drivers also recognise that speed limits are a maximum not a minimum, and they do not rely on others to avoid risks.

AVOID DRIVING IF YOU...

- Are feeling fatigued. You must not drive for more than two hours at a time without a break.
- Have flu.
- Feel tired.
- Are stressed or feel aggressive after, say, a bad day at work or a row at home
- Have consumed drugs or alcohol. Even some mild medicines such as a cold treatments, may make you feel drowsy.

Don't let your enthusiasm for driving tempt you into breaking the speed limit or driving dangerously. Advanced Drivers don't drive in this way, and always know what speed they are doing and what the maximum speed limit is. Timid drivers can be as dangerous as aggressive ones. Advanced Drivers drive decisively and always display a high level of self-control, having planned their next manoeuvre.

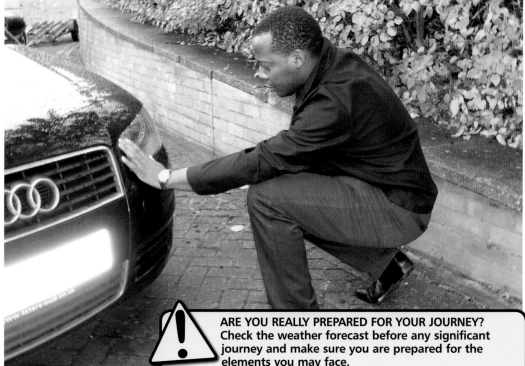

⚠ **ARE YOU REALLY PREPARED FOR YOUR JOURNEY?**
Check the weather forecast before any significant journey and make sure you are prepared for the elements you may face.
Radio, TV and internet are great sources of weather info.

ALWAYS ROOM FOR IMPROVEMENT

Whether you're a novice motorist or an experienced Advanced Driver, you'll find there's always room to improve your driving skills. Keep an open mind, be realistic about your limitations and always be prepared to learn from any errors you make.

YOUR REACTION TIME

Your thinking distance varies with the speed of the vehicle, your physical and mental condition and the degree of concentration applied. Even with lightning reflexes and at legal speeds, the distance your car covers before you can get your foot onto the brake pedal in an emergency is considerable. And that doesn't take into account the braking distance itself.

Your reactions are slow when you are tired, cold, ill or stressed. Drugs and drink also have a negative effect, but may actually make you think you're reacting more quickly than normal.

You have minimal visibility and about 0.15 seconds to stop at 30mph Back off!

If you suspect danger ahead, position your foot over the brake. This will save valuable milliseconds if the worst happens.

The graph below shows the distances it takes to react (not brake) at various speeds. It assumes a fast reaction time of just 0.65 seconds – many drivers would take longer to react to a hazard.

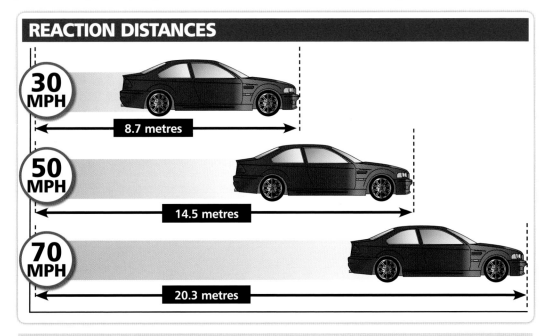

REACTION DISTANCES

30 MPH — 8.7 metres

50 MPH — 14.5 metres

70 MPH — 20.3 metres

OTHER PEOPLE'S REACTIONS

Always expect the worst from other motorists and try to understand what they are aiming to achieve. If you allow for poor observation and slow reactions, you'll find you're always prepared for the worst-case scenario.

When following other drivers, always apply the two-second rule (p.89). If you suspect they may not be totally focused on their driving, leave an even bigger gap to give you extra braking time. Tailgating is a common cause of collisions, it is dangerous and antisocial and can never be condoned.

Driving position

One of the most important aspects of driving a modern machine involves achieving the perfect driving position every time you get behind the wheel. This allows you maximum control over your car and will keep you more comfortable and alert on longer journeys. It's also the position most often adopted by racing drivers, especially rally and touring car drivers.

- Sit in the car with the base of your spine in the back of the seat to prevent back problems.
- Hold the wheel at ten-to-two or quarter-to-three. Keep your thumbs vertical.
- Whenever possible, adjust the steering wheel for improved control.
- Make sure your arms are slightly bent.
- Your legs should be slightly bent too, when your feet are on the pedals.
- The back of the seat should be fairly upright giving you a good view of the road ahead, mirrors, display and dials.
- Ensure that head restraints are adjusted so that they align with the top of your head. Make sure you know your vehicle's controls, including all light and windscreen wiper switches and parking/handbrake operation. Check the manufacturer's handbook for details.

Being too laid back, compromises your vision and your control of the car. It shows a lack of interest in your driving, and on long journeys is more likely to make you 'doze off'. Thousands of accidents each year are caused by drivers falling asleep at the wheel.

Position yourself too close to the wheel and, as well as looking slightly strange, you'll have less car control, your reaction times will be longer and, in the event of a accident, you could be hit by the airbag cover exploding out at over 200mph.

STARTING THE ENGINE

Take the time to read your vehicle handbook, and ensure you are familiar with how your vehicle operates.

1) Ensure that the handbrake is on and that the gear lever is in neutral – except in some automatics, which have to be in Park (P) to start the engine.

2) Turn on the ignition.
3) Depress the clutch (or footbrake if you're in an automatic).
4) Start the engine.
5) Make sure all the warning lights go out, and ensure you know what they refer to eg ABS, oil level, water level and

doors open. Check the manual if they stay on.
6) Make sure windows are clear and demisted.
7) Double-check and adjust your mirrors, set your heating/ventilation controls, satellite navigation and radio/CD before moving off.

Do you know what all these lights and controls are for?

WARMING THE ENGINE

Advanced Drivers value their cars and always seek to maintain the condition and performance of their vehicles. Mechanical sympathy is a big part of this. An Advanced Driver drives in a way that causes minimal stress and strain to their car. They know that over-revving a car from cold causes long-term damage

to the engine and gearbox, so they always warm their car up for a minute or so before driving off.

Modern fuel-injected cars don't suffer from flat-spots like old carburettor-engined cars. Drivers of older vehicles with carbs or a manual choke, should always take care on junctions and overtakes until

the engine is fully warmed up.

Always try to give your car time to cool down after a high-speed motorway run to avoid engine wear. This is especially important on cars fitted with turbochargers, as they can suffer bearing damage if the engine is turned off while the turbo is still red-hot following a fast drive.

MIRRORS

You should check all of your mirrors before every journey. All vehicles must be fitted with two or more mirrors, one of which must be internal.

- Ensure all mirrors are clean and clear.
- Position them to achieve the best views behind and to the sides of you.
- Make sure you are aware of any blind spots (see below)
- When parked in narrow streets and crowded car parks, fold your mirrors in to avoid them getting damaged by passing vehicles.

Ensure you are in the correct driving position before adjusting your mirror with one hand

"Consider taking a quick look over your shoulder to check that you haven't missed anything, before every manoeuvre you make."

HOW TO CHECK FOR BLIND SPOTS

Park on level ground and adjust your mirrors to take in the rear view. Glance into the offside mirror, or nearside mirror, then immediately look into the internal mirror. You will notice the blind spot immediately behind the rear quarters of the vehicle over your right or left shoulder. Be aware of this area but do not overcompensate by continually looking over your shoulders. Glance occasionally in each mirror to note the relative position of other vehicles as they approach from the rear, and note how that position changes.

Once on the road you can re-adjust your mirrors to minimise the blind spot delay. Consider taking a quick look over your shoulder to check there's nothing that you're unaware of before you make any manoeuvre.

SEAT BELTS AND THE CHILD RESTRAINT LAWS

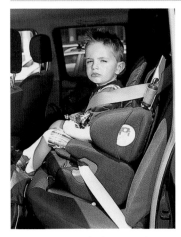 

Wear your seat belt every time you get in a car, even when you're in the backseat. If your seat belt shows any signs of wear replace it immediately.

The IAM recommends that children should always be restrained in a British Standards-approved child seat. 2006 legislation dictates that:
- Children under-three riding in the front must be in an appropriate child restraint – using adult belts is not allowed. When travelling in the rear, a child restraint must be used if available. Where there is a front restraint, but no rear, the child must travel in the front.

Rear facing baby seats should never be mounted in the front where there is an active passenger airbag.
- Children from three to 11 (or under 1.35 metres tall) travelling in the front of a car must use an appropriate child restraint if available. If not, an adult seat belt must be used. In the rear they must use an appropriate child restraint if available. (If one isn't available, the adult belt must be used where available.)
If an appropriate restraint or seat belt is in the front, but not the back, a child aged three to 11 years old must use that.

- Children aged 12-13 (or younger, but over 1.35 metres tall) must use an adult seatbelt if available.
- Children aged 14 or over must always use an adult seatbelt if available.

Isofix seat mounts are the safest way to secure a baby or child seat in your car. Most seat manufacturers make products designed specifically for use with these super-strong mounting points, which are common in many modern cars, and very easy to use. Common-sense always applies.

MOBILE PHONES AND DISTRACTIONS TO DRIVERS

Mobile phones may be an integral part of life, but it has been proven that using a phone whilst driving, massively increases your chances of having a collision.

The government has banned motorists from using handheld phones while driving (or even in a static car with engine on/ ignition keys in). The police can now stop and fine you and give you points on your licence.

If your phone fixation causes an accident in which someone is killed or injured, you could go to prison!

If you really do need to take or make calls when driving, get a hands-free kit and stop before engaging in protracted conversations – otherwise just turn your phone off and stop regularly to check your calls. Never send or read text messages when driving.

Also, always remind passengers who become a distraction, that you need to concentrate when driving.

Check the condition of your wipers regularly and before any long journey, especially in winter

UNTIDY VEHICLES

Having drinks cans, burger boxes and other rubbish rolling around the floor of your vehicle can cause serious problems. It's very important to keep all footwells tidy, especially the driver's side, as anything that could interfere with the accelerator, brake or clutch action is potentially lethal.

"Anything that interferes with your pedals could be lethal."

In-car driving aids

Gadget-packed modern cars give you much more to think about than ever before. Here are some of the cockpit devices available...

1. SATELLITE NAVIGATION

Sat nav systems are increasingly popular. If you have one, program it before setting off on your trip. Save time by adding all relevant destinations to the unit's memory. Where possible, position the screen close to your eye-line (but not obstructing your view) so that you can see it easily without taking your eyes off the road.

Always plan a route in advance and DO NOT rely on satellite navigation as your sole source of information. Occasionally one-way systems, fords or unclassified roads, for example, may not be accurately represented.

2. RADIO/CD/MP3

Select a CD or radio station before setting off. Advanced Drivers do not take risks by changing CDs or adjusting the radio on the move. Use your radio's traffic announcement system (the TA or TP button) to plan your journey around major hold-ups and traffic jams.

Some modern cars have stereos that can be controlled from the steering wheel. This minimises potentially dangerous distractions.

3. TV/DVD

Cars are increasingly fitted with TV screens and DVD players. Do not attempt to watch these when driving. Dash-mounted TV screens which may distract the driver are illegal. Consider buying headphones for rear passengers to avoid driver distraction.

4. CRUISE CONTROL

Cruise control takes a little getting used to, but is a useful tool, especially on long journeys, as it delivers a smoother ride and better fuel economy.

Consider using the SET function in speed-limited areas to avoid inadvertent speeding. Simply set the control to the relevant limit, then use RESUME to accelerate to the exact speed.

Turn your cruise control off in poor weather conditions as you'll need total 'manual' control.

5. ELECTRIC MIRRORS

Position all your mirrors carefully before setting off. Be aware of blind spots.

6. HANDS-FREE PHONE

Using hand-held mobile phones is illegal when driving. Some cars come with built-in hands-free systems, or they can be added. Ensure that your phone is in its cradle and the system functioning properly before you set off.

7. STEERING WHEEL CONTROLS

Cruise control, stereo, air-conditioning and even paddle-shift gear-change can often be controlled

As all vehicles have different specifications, ensure that you are completely familiar with all aspects of your vehicle's operation.

from a multi-function steering wheel. Ensure you are familiar with all these functions before you start your journey.

8. CLUTCH OR FOOTREST

Avoid 'riding' the clutch when you are driving, by moving your clutch foot on to the rest, or into the space to the left of the clutch.

9. ADJUSTABLE STEERING WHEEL

Position your steering wheel so that you are comfortable and can clearly see your dash display and the road.

SPEED CAMERA DETECTORS/LOCATORS

Some cars have built-in speed camera detectors and many 'after-market' systems are available. As Advanced Drivers always know the speed limit zone they are in and never exceed it, detectors are of limited use. They can however, give you early warning of other drivers' reactions when they spot a camera at the last second. Advanced Drivers do not rely on detectors/locators to manage their speed, but do make use of the useful driver information they provide.

ADVANCED CHECKLIST

- Maintain the vehicle regularly and keep it free of clutter.
- Ensure the driver's seat and head restraint are positioned correctly and hold the wheel in a 10-to-2 or quarter-to-three position, with your thumbs vertical.
- Keep the mirrors clean and correctly-adjusted.
- Familiarise yourself with all the controls of the vehicle by reading the manufacturer's handbook.
- Always wear a seat belt.
- Keep your windows clean and clear.
- Stop and turn off the engine before using a mobile phone.

EXAMINER CHECKLIST

- Is the vehicle in a roadworthy condition and road legal?
- Is the driver familiar with the vehicle controls?
- Is the seating position correct and head-restraint adjusted?
- Is the steering wheel adjusted correctly?
- Are all mirrors adjusted properly?
- Are driver and passenger seat belts on?
- Are windows clean and clear?

2 // THE BASIC PRINCIPLES OF ADVANCED DRIVING

Planned system

A GOOD INSTINCT TO HAVE

Approaching your driving in a systematic way will soon make good driving habits second nature. This is especially beneficial in complex driving situations. It enables you to manage all hazards in a planned, efficient, but flexible manner, where an ordinary driver might be flustered and panicked.

The early recognition of hazards such as physical features, the position and movement of other road users, and the changes in the road surface and the weather will give the all-important planning time that makes an Advanced Driver.

TIME TO REACT

Physical features include junctions, roundabouts, bends and hillcrests. Generally, they're simple to deal with systematically, but can be complicated by their layout and the movements of other road-users. If you then add a diesel spillage, ice, or heavy rain into the equation, you have a much more hazardous situation, and one that requires the use of a planned driving system to give you time to assess and react to all potential dangers.

Skill For Life incorporates an excellent five-part driving system, which you can apply to every driving manouevre you make. It's called IPSGA.

I P S G A

INFORMATION
Absorb Information: Always observe everything around you, including what's behind you.
Process information: Using your observations, plan how to deal with the hazards you've identified.
Give Information: Always give a clear signal when it will assist other road-users. Indicators are the most common method, but also consider arm signals, horn or headlights.

POSITION
Once you've signalled, position your vehicle correctly on the road. Consider re-checking your mirrors before changing course.

SPEED
Use your brakes, engine braking or acceleration sense to adjust your speed according to the hazard. Check your mirrors again.

GEAR
Once you're travelling at the right speed to negotiate the hazard, select the correct gear. (In some circumstances, you may need to change gear just before you finish braking.) Consider a final mirror check.

ACCELERATION
As soon as your car is on a straight course, after the hazard, accelerate to an appropriate speed.

IPSGA can be applied to any driving situation or manoeuvre. Practise it and IPSGA will soon become a natural thing to do.

It is intended to be used as a sequence, with the Information (observation) part overlapping the other four.

All aspects do not have to be applied slavishly, but should always be considered.

While it may appear long-winded here, when it's put into practice, it takes just a few seconds and soon becomes an instinctive behaviour.

As well as raising awareness of what's going on around you, it also ensures that your actions won't take other drivers by surprise. That said, you should keep an eye on other people to make sure they have seen you and are acting accordingly.

# of driving

INFORMATION
This part of the system should be continuously applied throughout the entire manoeuvre. Check your mirrors and signal before changing course, and maintain good all-round vision, looking out for pedestrians and cyclists as well as other vehicles.

In any manoeuvre such as this, always take extra care to look for motorcyclists.

POSITION
Check your mirrors. Carefully move the car towards the centre of the road, observing road width, lane markings and any potential obstructions.

SPEED
Check your mirrors. While signalling, brake progressively to a speed which will enable you to safely complete the manoeuvre.

GEARS
Once you're at the right speed, select the correct gear. Before turning, make a final mirror check.

ACCELERATE
Once you've made the turn and the wheels are straight again, accelerate to an appropriate speed.

This is just one example of IPSGA. To see how it applies to left turns and roundabouts, turn to Advanced Driving Methods on pages 61/62

THE IMPORTANCE OF IPSGA

Practise the IPSGA system regularly and it will soon become second nature. If you can do it without thinking, you'll have more time to concentrate on other elements of your driving. Planned IPSGA driving has many benefits, including saving lives, and saving fuel.

⚠️ Plan your approach to every junction. Consider slowing down earlier, so that the vehicles ahead have time to pull away before you arrive.

⚠️ Taking in and processing information throughout any manoeuvre is essential. You aren't going to miss this fast-moving yellow truck, but what about the motorcyclist following it?

"IPSGA should not be applied slavishly, but always considered."

Early planning and correct gear selection lets you maintain total control on your approach to a junction, making for a safer drive.

Know what is going on around you at all times and give necessary information, letting others know what you intend to do. The effective absorbing, using and giving of information is essential to Advanced Driving.

ADVANCED CHECKLIST
- Use the planned system of driving (IPSGA) every time you change speed or direction.
- Use all your mirrors effectively.
- Signal where necessary for the benefit of other road users, including pedestrians.
- Plan your application of the system.
- Use your gears to go and your brakes to slow.

EXAMINER CHECKLIST
- Does the driver use the system (IPSGA) consistently throughout the drive?
- Are the mirrors used in sequence?
- Are signals given only when necessary and at the correct time and place?
- Is the IPSGA driving system planned and acted upon in good time?
- Are braking, steering and changing gears systematic and separated?

Observation

Excellent vision and observation will help you stay out of trouble on Britain's crowded roads. To achieve superb observation takes commitment, thought and lots of practice

How many hazards can you spot in this typical urban scene?

To pass an L-test you only have to read a car number plate at 20.5metres (67 feet). To be an Advanced Driver, you'll need much better vision than that.

Most people's eyesight deteriorates very gradually, so they don't notice the effects, but research shows that millions of British drivers have poor eye-sight, and that can make them a danger to themselves, and you, every time they drive.

Poor eyesight can affect reaction times and spatial awareness, while restricted peripheral vision may cause a driver not to see a hazard at all.

Have an eye test every two years (or whenever you suspect there's been a deterioration in your vision) and always wear spectacles or contact lenses if an optician has recommended you wear them for driving.

To be an effective Advanced Driver, you must try to absorb as much information as possible every time you drive. There are dozens of things going on at any given moment and you have to instantly process all that information, focusing on those that are relevant and disregarding

Incredibly, this is all many of your fellow road-users can see!

those that are not. Of course, all drivers do this to a degree, but Advanced Drivers take it to another level, constantly assessing driving conditions, reading the road a long distance ahead, and making decisions accordingly.

FORWARD OBSERVATION

Almost all ordinary drivers only observe the road 5-20 metres in front of them, so, as well as missing most upcoming dangers altogether, at 60mph they have under a second to react if a hazard appears.

Advanced Drivers don't have this problem, they constantly scan the area closest to them, as well as the middle distance and all the way to the horizon.

One useful technique, is to immediately scan the next section of road, as far as you can see ahead, every time you round a bend or reach the crest of a hill. This early-warning system has massive benefits: you can often see what direction the road is going to take, identify up-coming hazards, see traffic jams early or spot potentially dangerous drivers or vehicles.

Your eyes are capable of long distance vision at the same time as short distance. If you look far ahead, you can still be aware of what is happening close to you. But if you look at something very close to you, like the rear of a car, you will struggle to see ahead.

Tailgating is the nemesis of forward observation. It severely limits your vision, often to a dangerous level, and means that any lorry or van driver in front of you may not even know you're there.

Advanced Drivers position their vehicle further back and slightly to the side, so that they can always see the line of traffic ahead of them, lifting their vision, but still being aware of the foreground to get early warning if the queue of traffic starts to brake.

'Lifting your vision' towards the horizon is one of the key advantages an Advanced Driver has over the ordinary driver.

What an ordinary driver focuses on

What an Advanced Driver focuses on

REAR OBSERVATION

Advanced Drivers obtain much more information from their rear-view mirrors than the average driver.

They don't just observe what's immediately behind, they use their mirrors to calculate speed and distance over a longer range, without, of course, neglecting what's going on in front of them. With practice, important information can be absorbed in a moment.

Always, be aware of your vehicle's mirror blind spots (see page 19). If in any doubt, have a 'lifesaver' glance over your shoulder.

When adjusting your mirrors, ensure part of your vehicle remains visible in them, as this gives a view of the traffic relative to your vehicle.

How to be a better driver

SELECTIVE OBSERVATION

Arguably the most important part of Advanced Driving is excellent observation. Drivers with great vision have to process lots of information quickly, so it's essential to develop a way of distinguishing between useful and irrelevant information. Here are some essential tips:

- Has the driver on the left at the junction ahead seen you? If you're not sure, move slightly towards the middle of the road, observing oncoming traffic and take your foot off the accelerator, keeping it hovering over the brake.
- Watch pedestrians carefully, especially children, OAPs (who may be deaf or partially-sighted) and anyone walking a dog. Always be prepared for the unexpected to happen.
- On a long straight, if a car some distance in front of you (say 200 metres or more) pulls out to overtake, you can be cautiously confident that there's sufficient time for you to overtake the car in front of you too.

- Changes in a road surface can have dramatic effects on car control. Look out for mud near farms, fields or construction sites, wet leaves on the road, streams of water running across the highway or even a change in the type of road surface (Tarmac, concrete, ShellGrip, etc.). All of these can upset a car's balance.
- A cluster of lamp posts in the distance may give early warning of a roundabout or major junction.
- In busy urban environments, use shop window reflections to observe approaching vehicles or changing traffic lights before you can see them directly, or to help you park.
- Observe parked cars ahead to see if there are any occupants. Be aware that a door may suddenly open, or, if the engine's running (look at the exhaust and lights) that they might suddenly pull out in front of you.
- Telegraph poles are often positioned on verges and therefore follow the course of the road. Use them as an early-warning system as to the twists and turns the road will take. Don't rely on them entirely, as they may track across a field (which you don't want to do!)

- Pay extra attention to stationary vans and give them a wide berth. Delivery vans stop often and someone might get out without looking.
- Give bicycle and scooter riders extra space.
- Look ahead for pedestrians' feet under the front or rear bumpers of parked vans, lorries and 4x4s. Is someone about to step out into the road?
- When behind a bus or school coach, be aware that when passengers start moving around inside, it's likely that a bus stop is coming up. Drop back ready to see if a safe overtake is possible.
- On hills, a cloud of exhaust smoke from an HGV suggests that it is changing down a gear and may be travelling much more slowly than other traffic.
- As you approach a large vehicle coming towards you, be aware that impatient drivers behind it may attempt dangerous overtakes.
- In bad weather look out for pedestrians whose vision may be limited by umbrellas, coat hoods or driving rain. Also, be aware of pedestrians in parkas and 'hoodies'.
- Allow sloppy or aggressive drivers more room. Drop further back from drivers attempting risky overtaking manoeuvres or who seem distracted from their driving. Never 'challenge' road-ragers.
- Notice whether the driver in front is paying attention to their driving, or are they distracted by a mobile phone or noisy kids, etc.
- Look through breaks in hedges and fences to spot upcoming potential hazards.
- When driving at night, use the headlight beams of other cars to assess their whereabouts, approach angle and even their speed. Headlamp beams of other vehicles may also give an indication as to where the road goes next.

Road signs

Advanced Drivers know what all road signs mean and update their knowledge from time to time with a glance through *The Highway Code*. Road signs are the shape they are because, even if you can't see the sign clearly, say in fog or heavy rain, you'll still know when you see a triangular sign that there may be a significant hazard ahead. So, do you recognise all the signs on this page?

ROAD SIGN RULES

- All warning signs are triangular.
- Advisory signs are rectangular.
- Round signs are 'the law' – you must do what they say.

Road signs are always there for a reason, so don't ignore them. They provide advanced information to help you avoid danger. You should be extra vigilant about some signs, like those warning of schools nearby, as they may indicate a 20mph speed limit ahead.

A pole with two or more signs on it should be read from the top, eg: below, the bend comes shortly before the junction.

A typical road junction in the UK is home
to numerous road signs. An Advanced
Driver knows what they all mean

ADVANCED CHECKLIST
- Develop your selective observation. What info should you act on and what can you ignore?
- Read and understand the meaning of every road sign.
- Use rear-view mirrors to observe where other traffic is and how fast it's travelling.
- Watch the traffic in front of the car you're following. This will give you early warning of potential hazards and general traffic movements.
- Observe activity in the middle-distance, as far as you can see ahead and scan laterally all around you.
- Get your eyes tested every two years or the moment you suspect any deterioration.

EXAMINER CHECKLIST
- Are mirrors used properly before signalling and manoeuvring?
- Are mirrors used frequently and effectively?
- Does the driver see, absorb and act on all road sign information?
- Does the driver lift their vision to the road ahead and show good anticipation?
- Are speed and distance judged accurately?
- Can the driver stop in the distance seen to be clear at all times?

Driving hazards

The UK's busy roads are full of potential dangers. Advanced Drivers spot these hazards early and take appropriate action

A hazard is anything that contains an element of actual or potential danger. That includes junctions, roundabouts, hillcrests and bends, as well as the position and movement of other road users and even the weather. Imagine combining all six of these elements in one scenario and you have a massive potential for danger.

To an Advanced Driver, any junction, say a roundabout, traffic lights or a right turn, is a hazard, not just a child running into the street, a blind bend or an accident black spot. This means that it is essential for you to position your vehicle correctly when dealing with them, giving you that one essential safety 'ingredient' – sufficient time to react.

"A hazard is anything that contains an element of actual or potential danger."

WHY YOU NEED TO THINK AHEAD

On pages 12 and 13 we showed you just some of the potential dangers you'll face every time you drive a car. To minimise your chances of being affected by adverse driving conditions, or other people's mistakes, you must take a planned and systematic approach to your driving.

This means you'll anticipate hazards, spot them earlier and allow enough time and space to avoid them all together. Even in the worst-case scenario, you'll give yourself enough time to take effective evasive action.
Thinking ahead means that every manoeuvre is made in good time and under control.

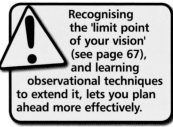

Recognising the 'limit point of your vision' (see page 67), and learning observational techniques to extend it, lets you plan ahead more effectively.

WHAT IS COMMENTARY DRIVING?

Commentary driving – describing aloud everything you see, think and do whilst driving – is a great way to hone your Advanced Driving technique.

On a busy road or in an urban environment you'll often find there is so much going on that you can't describe it all quickly enough – you simply can't keep up verbally. This proves how many thought processes a vigilant driver goes through on an everyday drive. Commentaries illustrate how much you are really seeing and the level of thinking involved, not just your actions.

Commentaries are not part of the test, but you may be asked to do one during your preparation, so it's well worth trying it out. Practise regularly and your observation, understanding and anticipation will improve immeasurably. Here's an example…

EXAMPLE COMMENTARY

This is a commentary from a small market town – imagine how busy a city would be.
"I'm turning right out of a concealed driveway on to the main street of a small town. Mirrors. Weather conditions and visibility are good, but because it's lunchtime, town looks quite busy.

"The cenotaph roundabout opposite is quiet. Mirrors. There are a number of parked cars.

"There is a zebra crossing in 50 metres which looks crowded. Mirrors. A cyclist and a motorcyclist are approaching it, along with a Vauxhall Corsa.

They may have to stop if someone crosses. Mirrors. The pavements are very narrow and there is a mother with a pushchair and two unrestrained children – one of whom is carrying a football.

Ahead, the market square looks quite busy."

Driving plans

The driving plan and driving system are key elements of the IAM *Skill For Life* challenge.
How you assess what's going on around you, and how you act on that information, are the key differences between Advanced Drivers and ordinary motorists

DRIVING PLANS: THE THREE SIMPLE QUESTIONS

WHAT CAN BE SEEN?
Plan your drive on what you can see ahead, to the rear, and all around you.

WHAT CANNOT BE SEEN?
Remember that danger can exist on every hidden section of road: in concealed junctions, driveways, around the next bend or even from a bridge above the road you're on!

WHAT MIGHT REASONABLY BE EXPECTED TO HAPPEN?
Keep a look-out for clues to dangers that may lay ahead, eg:
• Junction warning signs give early notice that a driver may be waiting to pull out ahead.
• Dustbins outside houses on a twisty road, mean that there could be a stationary dustbin lorry around the next bend.
• Loose hedge clippings or straw on a country road, warn that there could be a slow-moving tractor or combine harvester round the next bend.
• At night, a car's headlight beams will provide early warning of its arrival.
• Think about the actions of traffic you are following too.

What can be seen? Illegally-parked lorry causes 4x4 to make a potentially dangerous manoeuvre

What can't be seen? A hidden roadsign can distract as you try to see the warning

- Will that dump truck be turning into the construction site up ahead? Will there be mud on the road? Is it overloaded? Could something fall off it right in front of you?
- Will that brewery lorry pull in suddenly at the next pub?
- Don't follow buses too closely or you may get stuck behind them when they pull up at the next stop. Drop back a little and keep a look-out for the next stop, as it provides advanced warning of an opportunity to pass.
- Be constantly aware that other drivers could (and probably will) do something unexpected at any time. For example, lane discipline on

What might reasonably be expected to happen? These boisterous school kids could run out at any second

major roundabouts is generally poor and cars often swap lanes without any warning.

- Prioritise hazards in order of importance and deal with each one accordingly.

With these potential hazards in mind, drive within the limits of what you can see, never assume anything and plan for danger to emerge from obscured areas.

3 // ADVANCED CAR CONTROL

Steering

Excellent steering is at the heart of Advanced Driving. Here's how to do it properly...

FEED THE WHEEL

After passing the standard driving test, few people then pay attention to how they hold the steering wheel. This is a mistake, driving with one hand on the wheel and another on the gearstick seriously inhibits your ability to make fast and accurate changes of direction and could cause problems if a hazard suddenly appears.

The best way to steer on busy, modern roads is from the top half of the steering wheel. Keep your hands between the ten-to-two and quarter-to-three positions, feeding the wheel through your hands and ensuring that your hands never reach the 12 o'clock or 6 o'clock positions, as this can seriously reduce your control of the vehicle.

This standard grip offers excellent car control in all situations, and results in your hands being correctly positioned – directly opposite each other – on the wheel, allowing you to steer quickly and accurately in any direction.

If you find this technique slightly awkward, begin any turn with a pull motion, rather than by pushing.

Advanced Drivers maximise control of their vehicle by keeping their hands on the steering wheel for as much of the journey as possible. When adjusting the air-conditioning or tuning the radio they do it on straight carriageway, not on a bend, when they have full control of the car and when traffic is light, leaving plenty of space between themselves and the car in front.

OTHER STEERING STYLES

Crossed arms Avoid crossed arms as you turn the wheel. It seriously limits your ability to make quick steering adjustments or add more lock.

One-handed steering This denotes a lazy driving style and gives poor car control, increasing reaction times if a hazard appears.

Both hands at the top or bottom of the wheel This is a sign of a complacent or over-confident driver. It gives poor car control and affects your steering reaction times and accuracy.

Letting the wheel slide through your hands Letting the wheel spin through your hands as you exit a turn gives very little car control should a hazard arise.

ACCURATE STEERING

Driving a modern, well-maintained vehicle is not a white-knuckle ride and doesn't require an overly firm grip on the steering wheel. In most circumstances, a vehicle will hold its line with minimal input, and only small, regular adjustments are needed.

Many novice motorists drive their small hatchbacks as if they're piloting a double-decker bus or a huge lorry. They have little sense of spatial awareness and imagine their car is a metre wider and longer than it is. This can cause delays by holding up traffic and can even be dangerous in narrow streets where they leave very little room for traffic moving in the opposite direction.

You should strive to learn the size of your vehicle and where its 'extremities' are. This can be tricky with modern cars where the bonnet slopes steeply away, giving little clue as to where it ends. Being skilful enough to judge gaps and manoeuvre your vehicle accurately through them is an essential part of Advanced Driving.

STEERING SMOOTHLY

Advanced Drivers steer in a controlled and progressive way, making smooth changes of direction, rather than jerky turns that upset the balance of the car, and the passengers. Accurate and smooth steering requires planning.

This technique has its roots in motorsport. Racing drivers recognise that a controlled and smooth drive is faster and safer than an erratic, jerky one. Sudden steering inputs make for an uncomfortable drive and negate many of the efforts of the car's designers to engineer suspension and tyres.

For a really smooth drive, focus on your steering and turn the wheel progressively going into the bend, keeping the car settled and level.

Maintain a balanced throttle (neither accelerating or decelerating) through the bend as this makes the most of the car's grip and poise, helping it to hold its line better.

Using this technique means that passengers will hardly notice the turn at all, even when driving at speed.

MAKING A RIGHT TURN

······ Hand sliding ——Hand gripping

1) Slide your right hand towards the one o'clock position while gripping the wheel with your left hand.
   Take a grip with your right hand and pull downwards, letting the wheel slip through your left hand.

2) At the same time as your right hand moves towards the five o'clock position, slide your left hand down to the seven o'clock position, and then change your grip to this hand.

3) Push the wheel upwards with your left land, keeping the wheel moving continuously. At the same time move your right hand back towards the top of the wheel and repeat if you need to apply more lock.

"With this steering technique, passengers will hardly notice the turn at all – even at speed."

MAKING A LEFT TURN

······ Hand sliding ——Hand gripping

1) Slide your left hand towards the eleven o'clock position on the wheel while gripping the wheel with your right hand.
   Now grip with your left hand and pull down. Let the wheel slide through your right hand.

2) At the same time as your left hand moves towards the seven o'clock position, slide your right hand down to the five o'clock position, and then change your grip to this hand.

3) Push the wheel upwards with your right land, keeping the wheel moving continuously.
   At the same time move your left hand back towards the top of the wheel and repeat if you need to apply more lock.

STEERING WHILE MANOEUVRING

1) Position yourself comfortably, so that you have a good view behind you. Consider putting your left arm on the back of the passenger seat.

2) Grip the top of the steering wheel with your right hand. Use this hand to move the wheel.

3) Make sure that you don't forget to replace your seat belt if you have taken it off while you are carrying out your reversing manoeuvre.

STEERING MESSAGES

Experienced Advanced Drivers receive a lot of information through the steering wheel. Changes in road surface and the level of grip it provides are arguably the most crucial, but the condition of the vehicle's steering, suspension and tyres can also sometimes be assessed directly through the steering wheel 'feel'.

Power-steering systems often reduce this 'feel' (sometimes totally), but many modern cars are engineered to give good feedback which an Advanced Driver can benefit from.

When cornering, tighten your grip as you enter the bend, and always make gradual steering inputs in slippery conditions.

BASIC HANDLING CHARACTERISTICS

You don't need to be an engineering expert to have a worthwhile appreciation of a car's handling characteristics.

If you drive different types of cars: front-wheel drive, rear-wheel drive, mid-engined etc, you'll notice differences in their handling characteristics.

● Understeer happens when a bend is taken too quickly and the car 'ploughs' straight on, even though the steering wheel is turned. It is engineered into many front-wheel drive cars, because it is considered to be the safest option, as braking tends to put the car safely back on the straight and narrow.

● Oversteer is when the back end steps out, making the vehicle turn in more than the driver intended. It can lead to a total loss of control or a spin. Oversteer is most common with rear-wheel drive cars and can be controlled by an experienced driver using 'counter-steer', also known as opposite-lock.

● Some cars have neutral handling characteristics. When these are driven into a bend too quickly, both the front and rear wheels react in the same way and the car may 'slide' sideways, but as it's not changing direction totally, there is a degree of control for the Advance Driver to exploit.

ADVANCED CHECKLIST

- Always steer smoothly and progressively.
- Feeding the steering wheel through the hands ensures that one hand is always gripping the wheel.
- Holding the steering wheel lightly but with a firm grip, gives maximum feedback from the road.
- Begin all steering movements by 'pulling' from the top of the wheel, rather than 'pushing' from the bottom. This gives increased control.
- Practise steering accurately through tight gaps. This helps you develop a clear idea of your car's dimensions.

EXAMINER CHECKLIST

- Is steering smooth and accurate?
- Does the driver ever let go of the wheel altogether?
- Is the vehicle positioned properly?
- Is the steering wheel held correctly?
- Is the wheel passed through the hands?
- Are crossed-arms avoided, apart from when manoeuvring?

"Experienced Advanced Drivers receive a lot of information through the steering wheel."

Changing gears

Smooth, efficient use of a car's gearbox is an essential skill for Advanced Drivers to master, as it increases car control, performance, economy and ride comfort

TYPES OF TRANSMISSION

There are four main types of transmission or gearbox to choose from. They are...
● A manual gearbox with a clutch. These are the most popular choice in Europe as they're cheap and give excellent control. Most modern cars have five or six manual gears.
● An automatic gearbox typically has from three to

seven gears, which are changed automatically without the need for driver input or a clutch.
● Semi-automatic and Tiptronic gearboxes are increasingly popular. Many have a gear stick in the standard position, but don't have a clutch. When the gear stick is pushed or pulled to change up or down, the clutch

is operated automatically. Some modern cars also feature 'paddle-shift' similar to an F1 racing car. Levers on the steering wheel are pulled or pushed to change gear.
● Continuously variable transmissions (CVT) only require the driver to select forward or reverse. All changes are made automatically by the vehicle.

SMOOTH USE OF GEARS AND CLUTCH

A good gear change is so smooth that your passengers won't even notice it has taken place. To achieve this smoothness, you must select a gear that matches the engine speed and road speed, and you must use the accelerator and clutch skilfully.

As an Advanced Driver, your goal is to drive as smoothly as possible at all times. Drivers often get a false perception of how smooth their driving is, because they have the steering

wheel for support. Ask your passengers for an assessment of your driving smoothness, or watch them in your peripheral vision. If they are rocking around as you negotiate a roundabout or corner, your technique isn't smooth enough and needs more work.

When changing up a gear, release the accelerator and depress the clutch simultaneously, and only press the accelerator again as your foot is releasing the clutch.

Expert timing will produce silky-smooth changes every time.

When changing down a gear, you'll increase smoothness by matching the engine speed to the road speed with a brief blip of the accelerator.

Good gear changes are also good for your car (and wallet). They keep your clutch and gearbox in excellent condition for longer, and save petrol. Poor gear changes and 'riding the clutch' cause expensive premature wear.

For more accurate, smoother and professional-looking gear changes, have your thumb pointing downwards when moving the lever into the gears on the left-hand side of the gearbox ie: first, second and reverse...

... and keep your thumb pointing upwards when changing into third, fourth, fifth and sixth

GET THE RIGHT GEARS

Always select a gear that balances your need for economy, performance and mechanical sympathy.

You should always aim to minimise driving and mechanical inputs. For example, after a fast third-gear overtake, it's often best to change straight into fifth gear. This is called block changing (see page 46), and should be used wherever possible.

Always set off in first gear, as 'launching' in second can leave you in the lurch, should an unexpected turn of acceleration be needed. Selecting too high a gear will cause the engine to 'bog down', killing acceleration.

Turbocharged engines are very susceptible to 'bogging down' (called turbo lag) if you miss the engine's powerband by selecting a wrong gear. This can be very hazardous at junctions and during overtakes.

Diesel engines deliver their power and torque at much lower revs than petrol engines, and their powerband is much narrower – typically from 1500-4000rpm. This means that there is little point in 'revving out' a diesel engine, as above 4000rpm no extra power is delivered and fuel is wasted. Slick, well-timed gear changes will drop you nicely into the power band for the next gear, ensuring both good progress and economy.

Any issues can be avoided if you take the time to learn your engine's power-delivery characteristics. Knowing how it performs will produce a smoother, faster and more economical drive.

Use engine braking for steep hill descents, by selecting a low gear. This reduces strain on your brakes.

As a general rule, use the same gear to descend a hill as you would to drive up it, this delivers a good braking effect.

ECO DRIVING

The IAM has always recognised the value of economical driving. Block changing saves fuel when accelerating and decelerating, compared to working your way through all the gears.

Understanding your vehicle's power delivery and where its powerband lies, is also essential to maximise economy and performance. This allows you to get the most out of your engine at all times.

These techniques deliver a fuel efficient, and therefore environmentally-friendly, drive. For more fuel-saving tips see page 58.

BLOCK CHANGING

Block changing – changing gear from, say, third to fifth or fifth to second in one movement is an important part of Advanced Driving.

Advanced Drivers make excellent progress by applying firm acceleration wherever it is safe and applicable. This could often mean reaching a 60mph speed limit in, say, third gear after an overtake manoeuvre. What then is the point in changing from third to fourth and fourth to fifth just to maintain the same speed? This is an opportunity to minimise your driving inputs (and your fuel consumption) by changing straight from third into top gear, missing out fourth.

Likewise, on approaching a roundabout or junction, slow your speed, using either your acceleration sense (p.50) or your brakes, then select the best gear for your exit. This may well mean changing straight from fifth to second.

You should always aim to make gear changes after braking and before you turn the steering wheel. This produces a smooth, safe, progressive and economical drive, which your passengers will really appreciate.

⚠ **Advanced Drivers use their acceleration sense or their brakes to slow down – not their gears. This minimises engine wear and driving inputs and requires a more considered driving style.**

USING AN AUTOMATIC

Automatic and semi-automatic gearboxes, are now more popular than ever.

They allow you to focus on the road ahead rather than changing gear and you don't have to remove your hands from the steering wheel.

Modern automatics are increasingly performance-focused (many even have sports settings). For fast acceleration you use the 'kickdown' function. This is achieved simply by pushing hard on the accelerator.

As a rule, left-foot braking is best avoided. It is a tricky technique that's best left to Scandinavian rally drivers!

When coming to a halt in an automatic, leave the gearbox in Drive unless you are stopped for an extended time.

Finally, passing your driving test in an automatic vehicle prevents you from driving a manual car until you have passed a test in one.

COMING TO A STOP

Imagine you are driving through town at 30mph in fourth gear. You see the traffic lights ahead turn red, so you begin to brake.

Advanced Drivers should stay in fourth gear, then declutch just as they come to a halt. However, all cars react differently and you will eventually reach a point where the engine begins to labour and judder because you are in too high a gear for the speed. To prevent this juddering, you must depress the clutch progressively to stop the engine stalling.

Advanced Drivers should never let their vehicles free-wheel, however in this situation you must break that rule briefly, de-clutching and braking to a stop.

Once you are stationary, apply the handbrake, change gear into neutral, then select first gear shortly before you expect to set off again.

"Advanced Drivers never free-wheel, but in this scenario must break that rule briefly."

ADVANCED CHECKLIST
- Hold the gear lever properly.
- All gearchanges should be smooth, precise and well-timed.
- Where relevant, select gears with economy and the environment in mind.
- Smooth, slick down-changes require varied accelerator pressure to match engine and road speeds.
- Use your gears to control speed on steep hills and in slippery conditions.
- Overtaking requires planned gear-changing technique.
- With some automatics, consider using the transmission 'manually' where required.

EXAMINER CHECKLIST
- Is the gear lever held properly?
- Is the driver in the correct gear for every situation? (Consider Eco driving)
- Are engine and road speeds correctly synchronised when changing gear?
- Is the driver capable of engaging a gear without using an intermediate gear (ie blockchanging)?
- Are gears changed smoothly?
- Is the foot off the clutch between changes?

Speed and acceleration

Knowing when to use your car's power and when to take it easy are skills which every Advanced Driver has mastered. *Skill For Life* isn't about driving around at a snail's pace, it's about using power and acceleration smoothly and safely

WISE USE OF POWER

Power is nothing without control. This is true of all aspects of driving and a maxim the Advanced Driver lives by. A powerful sports car is at best wasted, and at worst deadly, in the hands of an amateurish or lazy driver.

Advanced Drivers never abuse their car's power. Instead they learn how the car delivers its power, then use their experience to make the most of it, driving as safely, smoothly and progressively as possible.

Firm acceleration is sometimes necessary – when joining a motorway from a slip-road or when overtaking, for example – but to make the best use of your car's power takes practice and an understanding of the way it delivers its torque (the force that creates acceleration).

Earlier, we touched on how being in the wrong gear at the wrong time can 'bog' the engine down, restricting the car's acceleration and possibly putting you in a hazardous situation. It's important to learn which part of the rev band delivers the most torque and acceleration. This will ensure you select the right gear for the conditions and the 'job' in hand.

Generally, petrol-engined cars deliver maximum torque (acceleration) between 4000 and 6000rpm. This means you may well need to be in a lower gear to 'hit' the powerband. Typically, you might need to change down to third gear to accelerate on a short motorway slip road.

Diesel engines on the other hand, produce their torque much lower down the rev range at anywhere from 1500 to 3000rpm. This reduces the need for changing down, but does mean that diesel engines run 'out of steam' much earlier than their petrol equivalents necessitating earlier up-changes if the driver wants to make good progress.

Variable valve-timing engines, like Honda's race-bred VTEC engine, are capable of very high revs (up to 9000rpm) and hence deliver their peak torque and power much higher.

Modern fuel-injected engines do not consume fuel when your foot is off the accelerator. Therefore the block changing techniques used by Advanced Drivers will save both money and the planet.

GRIPPING STUFF

Take note of how your car applies its power to the road. As acceleration transfers weight from the front to the back of the car, front wheel-drive cars will spin their wheels easily in wet conditions, and will even spin in the dry if you let the clutch out too quickly with the revs in the power band.

Rear-wheel drive cars gain traction under hard acceleration, as the car's weight is transferring on to the back wheels. That said, hard acceleration may still cause wheel spin, making the car unstable.

Advanced Drivers know that smooth power delivery is the key to speed, and that wheel spin is the arch-enemy of speed and control, so if your vehicle is fitted with traction control, do not turn it off.

Skilful use of the accelerator makes for a smooth drive and saves fuel

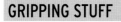

ACCELERATED LEARNING

Advanced Drivers have a highly-developed acceleration sense which means they have to use their brakes less than ordinary drivers. With their excellent observation and anticipation, they quickly assess the driving conditions ahead and use their expertise to make the necessary changes to their speed to produce a progressive, smooth and safe drive.

The accelerator should always be used progressively. For firm acceleration, begin by accelerating moderately. Then, once the car is settled, apply more throttle.

Use the same technique when decelerating. By easing your foot off the gas gradually at first, you'll produce a more controlled, smooth and economical drive.

The displayed speed limit is the maximum speed you should drive at. In this situation, 20mph would be too fast

TEST YOUR SENSE OF ACCELERATION

Here's a really useful way to test your sense of acceleration or deceleration.

Next time you're driving along at the national speed limit and see a 30mph or 40mph speed limit sign ahead, try to time the point at which you 'lift off' the accelerator, so that the car

reaches the speed limit sign at the correct speed, without the need to touch the brakes.

On twisty roads you can take this technique a stage further, by managing the speed of the car between bends with accurate use of the accelerator. This will limit the amount

of braking you need to do, producing a smoother, more satisfying drive, it'll make you a more precise driver and you'll save fuel. (See page 67 for information on the 'Limit Point of Vision' technique, a useful tool when developing your acceleration sense.)

"Good sense of acceleration makes for a great drive."

ACCELERATING ON BENDS

Advanced Drivers know that a car is most stable in a straight line under progressive, smooth acceleration. Things can go wrong when the car is in a turn and the driver accelerates

too harshly. For maximum stability and comfort, maintain a 'balanced-throttle' at a constant speed and a smooth line through the bend. (See Cornering on page 67).

ACCELERATION AND OVERTAKING

Make sure all your overtaking manoeuvres are carried out safely, smoothly and swiftly. If you have to push your car to the limit, or other drivers have to take avoiding action, it means you've left too little a safety margin.

Select the best gear for the overtake, bearing in mind your car's power delivery, to ensure it will produce the acceleration required. Avoid changing gear during the manoeuvre, as it increases the time you're exposed to danger.

SPEED

You will fail your Advanced Driving challenge immediately if you break any speed limits. Spot speed limit changes early using your observation skills, and stay in a gear that will help you to remain at a legal speed. For example, when driving in town at 30mph, third gear is often a good choice as it delivers decent acceleration when you reach the national speed limit again.

Speed limits show you the maximum speed you can drive at. In busy urban environments, or anywhere with many potential hazards – a busy city street with lots of parked cars, or outside a school or hospital – it may be advisable to drive even slower.

With smooth road surfaces and powerful, quiet cars, it can take serious concentration not to creep over the speed limit. Incentivise yourself by remembering just how difficult it is to enjoy your motoring without a driving licence!

One of the 'Golden Rules' of Advanced Driving is to always drive at a speed that allows you to stop safely within the distance you can see to be clear ahead. Don't ever be pressured into breaking the speed limit by drivers behind you.

Advanced Driving is not about driving slowly. Drivers who tootle along at 50mph on a busy motorway or 30mph on a clear country road can be just as dangerous and frustrating as speed demons. The skilled Advanced Driver looks to make good progress wherever possible by carrying out well-timed overtakes; smooth, progressive cornering and timely, controlled acceleration.

ADVANCED CHECKLIST
- Familiarise yourself with your vehicle's power delivery, so that you can make the most of the power available.
- Make sure you're in the correct gear and use as much power as is safe if overtaking.
- Accelerate smoothly, progressively and with economy in mind.
- Develop your acceleration sense. You'll use your brakes less, know instinctively when an overtake is on and drive altogether more smoothly.
- Use a balanced-throttle to keep the manoeuvre stable and smooth.

EXAMINER CHECKLIST
- Are speed limits adhered to?
- Is the use of acceleration excessive or insufficient?
- Is acceleration smooth and progressive?
- Is acceleration used at the right time and place, and with economy in mind?
- Does the driver make good progress and exercise proper restraint?
- Is the balance of the vehicle maintained in bends?

Braking

If you've ever been a 'nodding-dog' passenger in a car and got out feeling seasick, you'll know the effects of ill-timed and harsh braking. Achieving a smooth, progressive and effective braking technique will make every drive safer and more pleasurable... for everyone involved

SMOOTHNESS

Advanced Drivers brake progressively and smoothly. To achieve this, they must develop superb observation and anticipation skills, as this allows them to begin braking earlier, should any unexpected hazards arise.

Effective braking is a skill that requires practice. You should roll the pressure onto the brake pedal progressively; do most of the braking in the middle phase; roll off the brake again and then select the best gear to make good progress.

This method always produces the smoothest drive.

Practise this technique by attempting to produce such a smooth drive that your passengers don't even realise you are braking – decelerating gradually so that the nose of the car never dips.

Well-timed braking will usually make you faster from A to B. Take timing your arrival at a roundabout for example. Look well ahead and assess the traffic on the roundabout, then time your arrival so that

you don't have to stop. The cars that sped past you as you were decelerating early, will be at a standstill trying to find first gear as you slide past effortlessly and get straight back on the accelerator.

Keep every drive as simple as possible by not overlapping braking, steering and gear inputs. However, if driving conditions force you to do so, always overlap a gear change with braking, not steering as that would mean taking a hand off the wheel.

Planning your braking early makes for a smoother, more consistent drive and saves fuel

BRAKING DISTANCE

Total stopping distance is worked out by adding 'thinking distance' and 'braking distance' together.

The time it takes you to react is the main factor in 'thinking distance', while 'braking distance' will vary according to your speed, the road surface plus your vehicle's weight and the condition of its suspension, brakes and especially its tyres.

Memorise the overall stopping distances in the *Highway Code*, and remember that as your speed doubles, your stopping distance will actually quadruple!

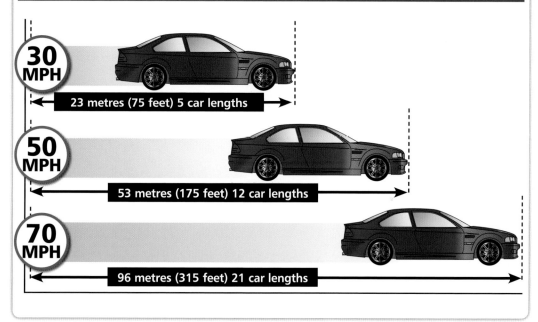

OVERALL STOPPING DISTANCE (THINKING DISTANCE + BRAKING DISTANCE)

30 MPH
◄— 23 metres (75 feet) 5 car lengths —►

50 MPH
◄— 53 metres (175 feet) 12 car lengths —►

70 MPH
◄— 96 metres (315 feet) 21 car lengths —►

Braking distances increase significantly in the wet, especially at speed. In testing, a Z-rated high-performance tyre at 70mph took five metres longer to stop in 1mm of standing water than in the dry. That's a whole car length… or a bus queue!

The same tests showed that the premium performance tyre brought the test car to a halt a massive 13 metres sooner than a budget performance tyre. In fact, the quality tyre stopped a distance of two car lengths shorter in the wet than the budget tyre did in the dry!

A tyre with a tread depth of 3mm or less, loses a considerable amount of its water-dispersing ability. This leads to much extended braking distances in the wet.

The moral of this story is that tyres are essential to your car's performance, and you should always invest as much as you can afford to buy the best tyres possible. Likewise, always make sure you have plenty of even tread on your tyres. The legal minimum is 1.6mm, but the 'progressive' driver should consider renewing his tyres before they reach that low level, as lack of tread massively effects wet braking and steering response.

Front wheel-drive cars wear out their front tyres much faster than the back ones, so you should consider swapping your wheels, axle-to-axle, about halfway through the life of the tyre. This will save you money and might even save your life one day.

JUDGING DISTANCE

It is essential to maintain a sensible distance between your car and the one in front. Under normal driving conditions, this is considered to be two seconds. (See picture opposite)

To measure it, watch as the car you are following passes a fixed point, say a bridge or shadow across the road. Start counting immediately (zero… one… two…). If you reach the point before two seconds has elapsed, you are too close.

On motorways and some dual-carriageways, you can use the white mileage posts, positioned every 100 metres along the side of the road, to judge your safe distance.

If the car behind you is too close, you should leave extra distance in front of you, to give yourself more braking time.

Unlike this driver, when driving slowly or completely stopped, keep your foot on the brake pedal. Your brake lights will warn any drivers following you

In effect, you are braking for the car behind you.

The same is true if you see an old, poorly-maintained or dilapidated motor looming in your rear-view mirror. Its brakes are unlikely to be as effective as yours, so sudden braking on your part could cause it to end up in your boot!

However tempting it may be, don't react aggressively to tailgaters, simply let them pass as soon as possible.

BRAKE IN A STRAIGHT LINE

Do your braking in a straight line before a bend – it keeps your car stable

Even with modern anti-lock brake systems (ABS), it is always best to carry out any firm braking in a straight line before making any steering changes. Any racing driver will tell you that using your brakes in the middle of a bend can upset the balance of the car and affect its handling.

If a situation arises that requires mid-corner braking, do so progressively to avoid locking the wheels.

As the most effective braking takes place just before the wheels lock-up, Advanced Drivers should develop a feel for this moment, and vary the brake pressure according to the road surface and conditions.

Only ever practise emergency braking in a safe place like on an old airfield or a skidpan.

Even firm braking can be done progressively, keeping the ride as smooth as possible.

Only a fool breaks the two-second rule!

Two seconds
One second

ANTI-LOCK BRAKES

Anti-lock brake systems (ABS) prevent a car's wheels from locking-up in an emergency situation, giving the driver steering control that otherwise would have been lost.

ABS works by releasing the brakes just before the wheels lock up, then quickly reapplying them. This process can be repeated hundreds of times every second, which means that the wheels never actually lock up. It is normal for this pulse to be felt through the brake pedal, and you should maintain your braking pressure.

Don't let ABS lull you into a false sense of security. Advanced Drivers should have such good observation and anticipation that they never need to rely on ABS.

EMERGENCY BRAKING

Braking as firmly as you can in an ABS-equipped vehicle is the quickest way to stop in the dry.

In wet or slippery conditions, a vehicle fitted with ABS may take longer to stop because the ABS system is working to maintain stability and retain steering control. In these conditions, the ABS can also emit a horrible 'graunching' sound. This is normal and should be ignored.

When driving a vehicle without ABS, locking up your wheels in an emergency-stop situation severely limits car control but is actually the quickest way to stop in a straight line in the dry.

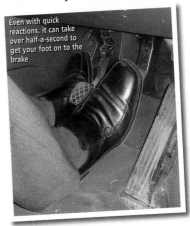
Even with quick reactions, it can take over half-a-second to get your foot on to the brake

BRAKE FAILURE

Modern vehicle braking systems are usually dual-circuit, so brake failure is very rare, but can still occur.

A slow hydraulic leak makes the brake pedal feel spongy and the brakes will start to lose their 'bite'. You may need to pump your brake pedal repeatedly to restore some pressure, and get any braking effect back.

If you recognise these symptoms, have your brakes checked immediately by a mechanic, before you lose your brakes altogether.

In very wet conditions, during a storm or after driving through a forded river, check your brakes regularly. Apply them progressively, but firmly to clear water from between the pad and disc. Don't be alarmed by any steam emitted, as long as it doesn't continue for more than a few seconds.

Should total brake failure occur, quickly change down through your gearbox and use the handbrake (whilst steering in a straight line) for maximum braking effect.

"Should total brake failure occur, quickly change down through the gears and use the handbrake."

BRAKE FADE

When driving progressively on twisty roads or steep hills, your car may suffer from a degree of brake fade. This usually happens when your brake discs and pads get very hot from repeated use and begin to lose their effectiveness. In extreme circumstances, the brake fluid may even boil, causing total brake failure.

Older cars and cars with drum brakes are more prone to this. Minimise the effect, by selecting a low gear to descend hills and use engine braking to slow the car as much as possible.

When stopping behind another vehicle, stay far enough back so that you can see its rear tyres on the Tarmac. This gives you space to manoeuvre and observe around it.

USING THE HANDBRAKE

Handbrakes should only be used when a car is static, but may be used in an emergency.

Advanced Drivers do not apply the handbrake every time they stop, but they do use it when stationary for longer periods, such as at traffic lights. This allows them to put the car out of gear and release the clutch, minimising clutch wear.

Make use of your handbrake to 'hold' the car when stopping on a hill, as constant 'slipping' of the clutch will cause damage.

When applying the handbrake, push in the button to prevent unnecessary wear on the ratchet mechanism.

ADVANCED CHECKLIST
- Always test your brakes before starting out on a journey.
- Allow for the reactions of other drivers when you brake.
- Know your car's braking ability. Always stay well within the limits of the car (and your own driving ability).
- When braking firmly, do it in a straight line as it keeps the car stable.
- Always consider your total stopping distance.
- Brake smoothly and progressively at all times.

EXAMINER CHECKLIST
- Is braking smooth and progressive?
- Are mirrors and signals used prior to braking?
- Are road and weather conditions taken into account?
- Does a lack of planning mean the driver has to brake twice when approaching a hazard?
- Does the driver avoid overlapping gear, brake and steering inputs?
- Is the handbrake release button pressed when the handbrake is applied?

Driving economically

The average British family now spends more money on cars and transportation than it does on food. So it pays dividends to drive with economy in mind

ECONOMICAL AND ECO-FRIENDLY DRIVING TIPS

With everything from fuel and insurance, to parts and maintenance costing more each year, it makes total sense to drive as economically and with as much 'mechanical sympathy' as possible. The IAM has always embraced this philosophy. The smooth, progressive style of the Advanced Driver results in savings in fuel and component wear, with the added bonus that most Advanced Drivers also get insurance discounts. This doesn't mean you drive everywhere slowly, skilled drivers make good progress, but do so without revving the engine unnecessarily.

Using less fuel saves money… and the planet.

Here are some useful tips to cut your expenditure, and the CO_2 you pump into the atmosphere…

● Planning ahead as you drive not only makes you more aware of hazards, it also helps you to drive smoothly and economically.
● Use acceleration sense. Do you go straight from the accelerator to the brake? Save fuel by planning ahead and gently letting the deceleration of the overrun bring you to a halt. There's no point in rushing up to a queue, then braking hard to a halt.
● Block changing uses your engine's power most efficiently and saves fuel.
● Obey speed limits. Driving smoothly at the speed limit will use up to 25 per cent less fuel.
● Don't slip the clutch or over-rev when manoeuvring.
● In a traffic jam, let the car in front open up a gap then try to keep moving smoothly at all times, rather than stop/starting.
● Keep your cruising speed constant. Use cruise control when possible (even in town).
● Always use as high a gear as possible, appropriate to your speed, and without compromising safety.
● Find out where your car's power band is (check in the manual). If peak power is at 5500rpm, for example, don't rev all the way to the rev-limiter at 6800rpm as you'll be wasting fuel and performance.
● Ask yourself: 'Do I really need to drive?' Short journeys of less than two miles cause the most pollution, as a straining, cold engine produces 60 per cent more pollution than a warm one.
● Plan the most direct route and drive at off-peak times if possible. Sitting in traffic means you are often doing zero miles per gallon. Think about car sharing, park and ride schemes or public transport.
● Regular vehicle servicing maintains engine efficiency and economy. Poorly-serviced cars can use 10 per cent more fuel.
● Checking tyre pressures regularly, minimises tread wear and fuel consumption.
● Minimise wind resistance by removing roof racks and carriers when not in use. Open windows increase drag and lower fuel economy. Remove unnecessary boot luggage, avoid heavy accessories and wide tyres that increase rolling resistance.
● Air conditioning lowers fuel economy by upto 15 per cent. Turn it off unless really necessary.
● Buy green fuel, and use less of it! Switch off the engine when stuck in traffic.
● Always try to reverse into parking spaces. When you start off again, driving smoothly away without having to reverse out not only saves fuel, it gives much better visibility.
● Don't fill your tank right up. You'll be carrying extra weight, which will reduce fuel efficiency.

Advanced Drivers spend less time
doing this than ordinary motorists

DIESEL v PETROL

A diesel engine gives better
fuel economy than its petrol
equivalent. That doesn't always
mean they'll save you money.

Most diesel cars cost more to
buy than their petrol-powered
counterparts and many require
more frequent oil changes.
These factors add to the total
running cost and mean that
you typically have to drive at
least 20,000 miles a year to
'pay back' the extra investment
through fuel savings.

Manufacturers are making
very economical small petrol
engines these days, so the
difference when compared to
diesel consumption is much
less. Mind you, smaller-engined
cars with their lower gearing
have to work much harder to
maintain higher speeds, so they
may not be a good choice for
those who regularly make long
motorway journeys.

SAFETY v ECONOMY

Never put fuel economy before safety. Driving significantly slower
than the conditions demand, for the sake of fuel economy, can
make you as much of a hazard as someone driving too fast. People
in the queue behind you may get impatient and take unnecessary
risks to overtake. Advanced Drivers are considerate drivers.

ADVANCED CHECKLIST
- A planned drive is an
economical drive.
- Good use of acceleration
sense, block changing and
knowing your vehicle's
power delivery all help to
save fuel.

EXAMINER CHECKLIST
- Does the driver have
a reasonable sense of
economy, avoiding
excessive revs and
unnecessary braking?
- Is driver anticipation
good enough to produce
a dividend in economical
driving?
- Is the right balance
struck between making
good progress and
achieving good economy?

4 // ADVANCED DRIVING METHODS

Road basics

If you master all the fundamental driving techniques, to the point where they become second nature, you'll have more time to hone your Advanced Driving skills. This chapter gives you the essential information to achieve this goal

"A massive 95 per cent of car-related collisions at junctions are caused by driver error."

JUNCTIONS

The majority of car-related collisions occur near T-junctions, crossroads, side turnings, roundabouts or forks. A massive 95 per cent of them are caused by driver error.

By using the IAM's Advanced Driving techniques and knowledge, and by developing a systematic approach to your driving (IPSGA, page 24), you will massively reduce the likelihood of such an 'accident' happening to you.

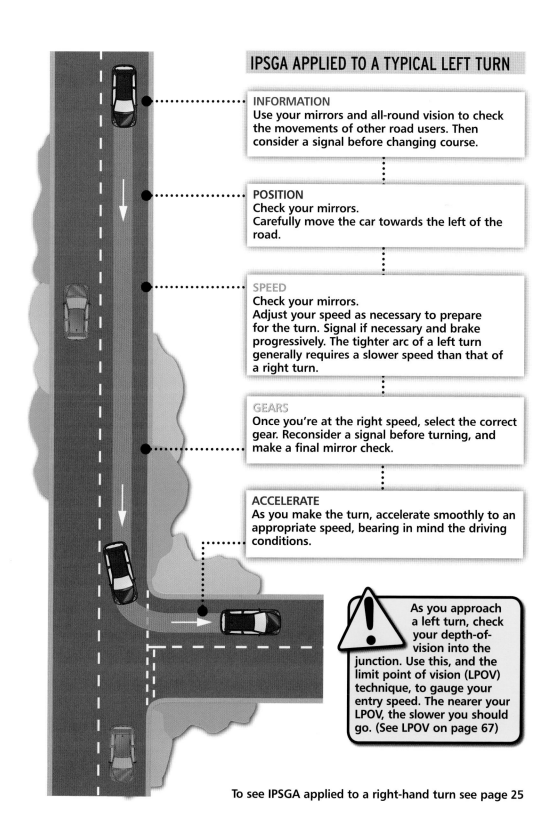

IPSGA APPLIED TO A TYPICAL LEFT TURN

INFORMATION
Use your mirrors and all-round vision to check the movements of other road users. Then consider a signal before changing course.

POSITION
Check your mirrors.
Carefully move the car towards the left of the road.

SPEED
Check your mirrors.
Adjust your speed as necessary to prepare for the turn. Signal if necessary and brake progressively. The tighter arc of a left turn generally requires a slower speed than that of a right turn.

GEARS
Once you're at the right speed, select the correct gear. Reconsider a signal before turning, and make a final mirror check.

ACCELERATE
As you make the turn, accelerate smoothly to an appropriate speed, bearing in mind the driving conditions.

As you approach a left turn, check your depth-of-vision into the junction. Use this, and the limit point of vision (LPOV) technique, to gauge your entry speed. The nearer your LPOV, the slower you should go. (See LPOV on page 67)

To see IPSGA applied to a right-hand turn see page 25

IPSGA APPLIED TO TURNING RIGHT AT A ROUNDABOUT

INFORMATION
Check your mirrors and use your vision to identify any hazards before considering a signal to change course.

POSITION
Check your mirrors and approach the roundabout according to which exit you plan to take.
  When turning right, carefully move the car towards the centre of the road.

SPEED
Check your mirrors. Decelerate smoothly to a speed that's appropriate for the turn ahead and the movements of other road users.

'Brakes are for slowing, gears are for going!' Advanced Drivers use this mantra to remind themselves of the correct way to decelerate. Use your brakes to slow your vehicle, then, once you have reached your target speed, block change into the correct gear to progress. Don't use your gearbox to slow yourself down.

GEARS
Once you're at the right speed to enter the roundabout, and before turning, select the correct gear and reconsider a signal. Make a final mirror check.

ACCELERATE
Choose an appropriate gap in the traffic and accelerate smoothly onto the roundabout, constantly checking all your mirrors and reconsidering signals. Always avoid disrupting the flow of other traffic.

POSITION
Check your nearside mirror, reconsider signals, then move to the left-hand lane in time for your exit.
  As you turn off the roundabout, accelerate smoothly to an appropriate speed, bearing in mind the driving conditions.

ROUNDABOUTS

Always drive in a way that allows you to change your plan if a signal is ignored

Correct positioning and signalling are crucial at roundabouts, and should always be complemented by a decisive but safe entry into the traffic flow.

Advanced Drivers calculate the speed and flow of traffic on and near the roundabout as they approach. They then attempt to time their arrival with a gap in the traffic, so that they don't have to stop, and don't cause an obstruction to other traffic.

A slightly slower approach often allows unobstructed progress, meaning they negotiate and exit the roundabout much quicker than the driver who raced up to the line only to be forced to stop.

In light traffic, you should only have to reduce your speed very slightly to enter the roundabout, but always bear in mind that other drivers at the previous entry may be thinking the same thing.

Always be vigilant and never assume that other drivers will do as their signalling suggests.

MINI-ROUNDABOUTS

Single mini-roundabouts are rarely a problem, but bunch a series of them together and the average driver seems to lose the plot completely – creating a real hazard.

Approach a cluster of mini-roundabouts one-at-a-time and treat each one individually. They should pose no threat to the Advanced Driver, other than the need for increased awareness of other drivers' behaviour.

Always be safe, observant and decisive, and, where possible, avoid putting a wheel into the central white circle.

SIGNALLING AT ROUNDABOUTS

On standard roundabouts, follow the *Highway Code*, unless lane markings instruct otherwise.

TURNING LEFT (FIRST EXIT)
Get in the left-hand lane and signal left on your approach. Continue to indicate until you reach your exit.

STRAIGHT OVER (SECOND EXIT)
Approach the roundabout in the left-hand lane and stay in that lane once you're on the roundabout. Signal left once you have passed the exit before yours.
Use advanced observation to see if the left lane is busy. If it is, consider using the right-hand lane. Use the same technique on the roundabout, but be extra observant, making good use of nearside and offside mirrors, when exiting.

TURNING RIGHT (THIRD EXIT)
Signalling right, take the right-hand lane into the roundabout and stay in that lane once on the roundabout. As you pass the exit that precedes yours, use your mirrors, indicate left and, observing carefully, move across to exit the roundabout.
  The number of lanes entering and exiting a roundabout affects your approach and signalling. Use your indicators to confirm your intentions and position your vehicle decisively.

Consider indicating right on a roundabout if your exit is past the '12 o'clock' position. Check that your exit is clear before committing to a manoeuvre and remember that direction arrows on roundabout approaches are usually for advice only.

TURNING RIGHT AT CROSSROADS (OFF THE MAJOR ROUTE)

Turning right at a crossroads can be one of the most confusing manoeuvres on Britain's roads, especially when an oncoming driver is also trying to turn right.

Problems can arise when drivers treat the manoeuvre differently – some trying to pass nearside-to-nearside, others offside-to-offside.

Advanced Drivers obey the Highway Code and always endeavour to pass offside-to-offside – they drive past the oncoming car in the junction in order to turn right behind them. This gives a clear view of approaching traffic.

Occasionally, road markings, traffic conditions, or the actions of the oncoming driver, might prevent you from doing this, so always proceed decisively, but cautiously, remaining aware that other drivers may not do what you expect them to.

CROSSROADS AND T-JUNCTIONS

Here's what to do at a junction where you are on the minor route, or where neither route has precedence.

• Pay extra attention to your speed, making sure you stay correctly positioned on the road.
• Check your mirrors, then signal if necessary, before braking early.
• Once stopped at the junction, consider using your handbrake if conditions mean you'll be stationary for a while, or you are on a slope.
• When there are no lane markings, position yourself positively. Indecision, or 'hedging your bets' by driving between imaginary lanes can confuse other drivers and cause unnecessary danger.
• Stay close to the nearside if you're turning left. When turning right, stay as close as is safe to the centre line.
• Make sure you are aware of the intentions of drivers at the road opposite before you begin to pull out.
• Always be patient. In heavy traffic, don't take risks by accelerating in to too small a gap. The actions of an Advanced Driver should never cause other drivers to brake.
• Don't assume that a flashing indicator means the driver will definitely make the manoeuvre he is signalling. He may have left it on by accident, or he may be confused and intend to take the turn directly after yours. Only pull out, when the other driver begins his turn.

If driving on a main road...
• Being on the major route at a junction doesn't mean you can do exactly as you like. Pay attention to other road-users

> **At junctions, is the other driver looking at you and are they aware that you are there?**

and always expect the worst from them, such as unsignalled manoeuvres, late braking and indecisiveness etc.
• On a main road, when approaching a junction where a car is waiting, try to observe the driver. If you are not sure he's seen you, take your foot off the accelerator and position it over the brake.
Also consider adjusting your position on the road, to give yourself vital fractions of a second to avoid a collision should he pull out in front of you unexpectedly.
• Advanced Drivers are considerate, but they never put courtesy ahead of practicality and safety. For example, they only let someone out of a junction if it won't cause undue braking by drivers behind them.

TRAFFIC LIGHTS

When approaching traffic lights, stop at or just before the stop line, then apply the handbrake and select neutral. Never pull up too close behind other traffic at lights – always leave yourself enough room to manoeuvre around them should they stall or breakdown.

At lights, try to keep an eye on the lights controlling the other routes. As soon as they turn amber, consider selecting first gear and prepare to release the handbrake, as your lights should go green in the next few seconds.

If you can't see the other lights, look for signs of the traffic slowing as their lights go to red. Use this anticipation to your advantage, but never move off before your lights turn green.

This advanced observation at traffic lights can speed up your progress. Look ahead and if there are several lanes, choose the lane of least 'resistance' – the one with less traffic in it, or the one without the slow-moving lorry or bus. Often the inside lane is empty which not only gives you a clear run, but also means you won't get held up by other traffic that will have to stop to turn right.

Observe the traffic you can see beyond the lights. Often lanes will merge. Aim for the lane that lets you make the best progress.

Time your arrival at traffic lights when they are at green. If you see a red light ahead, lift of the accelerator to delay your arrival, instead of 'steaming' up to the light and having to stop dead and change gears.

If you accidentally get in the wrong lane at lights, do not force your way into the correct lane. If someone lets you in, that's great, otherwise continue in your current lane, then turn around and retrace your route.

Finally, always be aware of drivers running red lights, as this trait is increasingly common on today's crowded and stress-filled roads.

Making well-timed, intelligent and planned progress on busy roads, is a uniquely satisfying experience – especially when you slip effortlessly passed the high-revving, push-in-at-any-cost driver who rocketed by you moments earlier only to end up in the wrong lane at the lights. Genius!

ADVANCED CHECKLIST
- Remember all junctions are hazards.
- Always consider signalling well in advance of a manoeuvre and take up the correct road position decisively.
- Pull away from a junction only when it's completely safe to do so.
- If you expect to be stopped at a junction for a short while, apply the handbrake and select neutral.
- On right turns at crossroads, pass oncoming traffic offside-to-offside before making your right turn. Occasionally road-markings or traffic conditions may prevent this.
- Always select the correct lane and signalling procedure when approaching and negotiating roundabouts. Your entry and exit should be decisive, well-observed and safe.

EXAMINER CHECKLIST
- Are signals, signs and road markings observed and obeyed?
- Is the correct road position taken up early when approaching a hazard?
- At a STOP sign does the driver stop and consider applying the handbrake?
- Are roundabouts negotiated safely, with a well-timed approach, good position and signalling, plus a confident entry and exit?
- Is sound judgement of gaps in traffic used when negotiating all hazards?

Cornering

Superb cornering is a satisfying skill to master. Here's how to do it...

Many aspects of Advanced Driving are exhilarating, but smooth, progressive and safe cornering is arguably the most enjoyable.

Advanced Drivers handle corners in a prepared and precise way, with superb observation, great planning, a good line through the bend and a progressive exit. These are crucial elements that raise driving standards above those of the everyday motorist.

Even an innocuous-looking corner requires real concentration to stop it becoming a hazard.

WHAT IS THE LIMIT POINT OF VISION?

The limit point is the furthest point ahead at which you have a clear view of the road surface. On a clear, level road this is the point at which the right and left-hand sides of the road appear to meet.

Advanced Drivers always drive at a speed that allows them to stop (on their own side of the road) within the distance they can see is clear – that is the distance between them and the limit point.

This determines how fast you can drive. The further away the limit point the faster you can go, as you have more room to stop in – and vice versa.

This applies to junctions as well as bends.

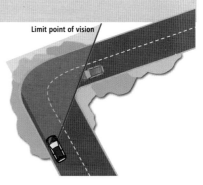

Limit point of vision

Limit point of vision – the furthest point that you can see clearly around a bend or obstacle

Match your velocity to the speed the 'limit point' moves away from you, providing you can stop in the distance that you can see is clear.

If you watch the limit point as you approach a bend or junction, you'll notice that it may move. If it moves towards you, slow down, as the bend or turn is tightening. If it moves away from you, it means the road is opening up. This 'limit point analysis technique' involves matching your speed to the speed the limit point of vision moves, accelerating or slowing your vehicle accordingly.

Using this method ensures the right choice of speed and the correct gear selection. This will enable you to maintain your vehicle's balance throughout any turning or curve.

The car will then be on the correct side of the road in a balanced and controllable state, and you will be able to stop in the distance you can see to be clear.

HOW TO CORNER USING IPSGA

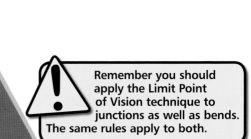

⑥

⑤

④

③

②

①

> Remember you should apply the Limit Point of Vision technique to junctions as well as bends. The same rules apply to both.

①

150 metres from the bend in the road and the Limit Point of Vision is moving towards you. Slow down.

②

You're 100 metres from the bend. You've slowed down and the LPOV is static. Maintain your speed.

③

50 metres from the bend. The LPOV is still static. You're at the correct speed to negotiate the bend.

④

40 metres from the bend. The LPOV is just starting to move away from you as the bend opens up.

⑤

You're right on the bend now. The LPOV is moving away from you, so you can consider accelerating.

⑥

Exiting the bend, the LPOV moves away from you. Accelerate with caution as the road drops away.

HANDLE ANY BEND LIKE A PROFESSIONAL USING THIS CORNERING TECHNIQUE...

Always observe as far ahead as possible to ensure that the road is clear. Use the 'Limit Point of Vision technique' (page 67) to maximise your observation and to manage your speed on approach to a hazard. On a rural road this is the point where the two verges or hedges appear to meet. This technique gives you valuable extra seconds to stop if a hazard appears.
1) On approaching any corner, check in your mirrors to see if another vehicle is approaching fast from behind and planning a possible overtake.
2) Position your car correctly on the road – move slightly to the left hand side of your carriageway on right-hand bends (but mind the verge, hedges etc), and slightly out towards the centre of the road on left-handers (but don't cross the white line or hit the cats'-eyes unless you have excellent visibility through the corner). This repositioning increases your view (limit point of vision) through the bend and makes for smoother steering and progress. Never position your car so far over that it unnerves other road users.
3) Manage your speed so that you can take the corner safely and progressively. Brake in a straight line and remember your speed must allow you to stop within the distance you can see to be clear in relation to the limit point of vision.
4) Look out for potholes and drains, or anything that could affect your cornering line. Continually reassess your limit point of vision and adjust your speed if necessary.
5) Select the correct gear to maintain the drive through the corner. Do it after you have finished braking and before you begin to turn in.
6) Steer into the corner with a progressive movement, not a jerky motion. Smooth steering keeps the car stable and balanced, helping you to maintain your speed right through the bend.
7) As you turn in and the car settles, apply a balanced throttle – just enough to keep your speed steady, but not be enough to accelerate.
8) As the road appears to open up and you are able to straighten the steering wheel, accelerate progressively bearing in mind the driving conditions.

CORNERING FORCES

Almost all crashes on corners are a result of reckless driving. Other factors, such as bald tyres and slippery road surfaces, are sometimes catalysts, but usually the driver is to blame due to poor observation, poor planning or too high an entry speed into the bend.

When cornering too quickly, a car will often skid straight on even though the steering wheel is turned – this is called understeer (See page 42).

Taking a left-hand bend too fast could easily result in you crossing the centre-line straight into oncoming traffic, while a tighter-than-expected right-hander might well see you on the verge, in a ditch or, worse still, colliding with a tree. Even minor changes in road surfaces can have a dramatic effect on the handling and stability of your car, especially at speed or when cornering. Unusual cambers (a deliberate sloping of the road to aid drainage) can assist you on left-hand bends, but work against you on right-handers.

Always observe the road surface you are on, adapting your speed and position accordingly.

BRAKING IN A CORNER

Always complete your braking, by achieving your target speed, before you turn into a bend. This is the safest, smoothest and most progressive way to drive and a technique used by racing drivers. Braking too late, once you've entered a corner, can upset the car's stability, even causing a total loss of control. Late braking also uses more fuel.

Where acceleration sense can't be applied, use your brakes briefly and smoothly between bends.

Where there is no straight 'braking zone' between bends, Advanced Drivers look for a brief opportunity where they swap between left-hand and right-hand steering to use their brakes without unbalancing their car.

Good observation should mean that you never have to brake 'late', once you're in a bend. However, if you are forced to brake in such a situation, do it smoothly and progressively.

ADVANCED CHECKLIST
- Always negotiate corners at a speed that allows you to stop within the distance you can see is clear (Limit point of vision).
- Complete any braking and gear changes before turning into a corner.
- If driving conditions allow, always position your car for the best view through the corner.
- Avoid sudden braking or harsh acceleration on bends.

EXAMINER CHECKLIST
- Does the driver consider road surface conditions when selecting their speed and line through a corner?
- Is the right choice of speed made?
- Is the correct gear selected to match the speed?
- Does the vehicle remain balanced throughout the bend?
- Is the car positioned correctly on the road throughout the entire cornering manoeuvre?
- Is steering smooth and progressive?

Overtaking

A well-timed, well-executed overtake is both satisfying and safe. Advanced Drivers use tried and tested techniques to perfect the fine art of overtaking

Is the overtake you're about to make really necessary?

DO YOU REALLY NEED TO OVERTAKE?

Ask yourself whether any overtake you are about to attempt is really necessary and worthwhile, and you'll soon discover that you have a more enjoyable and smooth drive.

What's the point in exposing yourself to unnecessary danger to jump one or two places up a queue of traffic? At best, you'll only arrive at your destination a few seconds earlier!

Instead of getting agitated, drop back, relax (not too much!) and enjoy the ride.

The bullying driver, who speeds up the wrong side of the road – only to cut up other drivers when he forces his way back in to avoid on-coming traffic – is a danger to himself and everyone else.

If you find a dangerous tailgater following too close behind you, don't react aggressively. Rise above the 'agitation', and make it as easy as possible for him to get by. The further away he is from you, the better.

Where an overtake is justified – for example, when you're following a slow-moving vehicle on a country road – you should carry out the manoeuvre as safely, decisively and quickly as legally possible.

Before beginning the manoeuvre, assess whether the vehicle may be turning off soon (a post van, milk lorry or tractor) and whether the overtake might be easier further down the road, if it widens or straightens.

If you're overtaking a vehicle with poor rear visibility, make sure the driver knows your intentions. Briefly beeping your horn or flashing your headlights may help. This is particularly advisable when passing distracted car drivers, lorries, caravans or tractors and trailers, as these slower-moving vehicles can turn very quickly, often without braking.

WHEN TO OVERTAKE

Every advanced overtake requires planning, quick thinking and decisiveness. Ask yourself these questions before you attempt any overtaking manoeuvre:

- Is their sufficient clear road to carry out the manoeuvre safely? Is anyone ahead slowing down or turning right?
- Does your car have enough acceleration to pass safely?
- Which gear will provide the best acceleration to complete the manoeuvre?

- Will you get a better overtaking opportunity soon?
- Is the vehicle in front hiding another vehicle that may block your attempts to pull-in?
- Beware of slow moving vehicles, they can turn quickly.
- Are there any concealed hazards such as obscured lay-bys, side turnings, entrances, buildings or gates?

Never overtake near a junction, even one that looks clear. The vehicle you're passing might turn without warning, or someone might pull out. When joining a main road, a lot of ordinary drivers only take the time to look right – this is the cause of numerous high-speed accidents.

- Observe around and underneath any vehicle you're passing, to check all is clear in front of it. Often, shadows are a good way to judge whether, for example, a motorcycle is being obscured by a large lorry.
- Never make risky overtakes. If in doubt, stay back.

1) THE OVERTAKING POSITION

Consider selecting a lower gear when your long-range observation indicates that an overtake may be on. Close in gradually on the vehicle in front, until you achieve the 'overtaking position'. Move towards the centre line to maximise your view. If the overtake does not come off, drop back again and return to a higher gear until the next opportunity arises.

2) THE TAKE-OFF POSITION

When an overtaking opportunity arrives, move carefully and smoothly to the other side of the road to increase your view, before you commit to the manoeuvre. All this takes just a second for the Advanced Driver to assess. If everything is clear, accelerate quickly past the vehicle. If conditions are not right, drop back in behind the vehicle quickly and smoothly.

THE OVERTAKING TRIANGLE

Police Advanced Drivers are taught a three-point overtaking method called the overtaking triangle. It defines the best line to take throughout any overtake manoeuvre and is the safest and quickest way to pass another vehicle. Below you can see exactly how it works in three easy steps. Combine this technique with excellent observation, anticipation and car control, for fast, efficient and safe overtakes everytime.

Check your mirrors before any overtake manoeuvre – and always be aware of blindspots

3) THE RETURN POSITION
The final part of the overtaking triangle returns you safely back to your side of the road, completing the manoeuvre.
Steer your vehicle to the left-hand side swiftly and smoothly, and in as straight a line as possible. Take care and use your mirrors to ensure that you do not cut in too quickly on the vehicle you have just passed.

"Every advanced overtake requires planning, quick thinking and decisiveness."

Before you attempt any overtaking manoeuvre – THINK!
• Is there enough space to get by?
• How fast is the oncoming vehicle in the distance travelling?
• Are there any buildings with entrances, side turnings or lay-bys?
• Is the vehicle you're about to pass concealing any other vehicles?
This extra attention to detail could save your life one day.

COMMON OVERTAKING MISTAKES

Advanced Drivers practise their skills to avoid making the following basic mistakes…

● Incorrect gear selection limits your acceleration and lengthens the time you are exposed to danger. Get to know your car's power delivery, for safe, smooth overtakes.

● Carrying out an overtake, only to discover another vehicle blocking your return position. This leaves you exposed to danger and having to 'bully' your way back in.

● Failing to notice buildings, junctions, lay-bys or entrances, that may spell danger.

● Failing to consider that another driver might be planning to overtake when attempting to pass two or more vehicles.

● Planning and executing your overtake so poorly that it has to be aborted at a very late and dangerous stage, eg: while alongside the other vehicle.

● Gambling on what traffic may or may not come around the next bend or on the speed of approaching vehicles. Optimism and risk-taking are not part of Advanced Driving – always consider the worst-case scenario.

● Driving much too close behind the vehicle you're about to overtake. Drivers of low-powered cars are often tempted to do this.

● Waiting too long in the overtake position, on the off-chance that an opportunity may arise. Minimise time spent in this vulnerable position.

● Forcing other drivers to react to accommodate your poorly-timed overtake.

● Pulling out to overtake without using your mirrors, only to discover a faster vehicle is already committed to a manoeuvre behind you.

The truck looks fully-loaded, so hang back and move out into the take-off position early, keeping an eye on his load

Don't move alongside the truck, until the car in front has passed it. Always ensure you have options and escape routes. Don't allow yourself to get blocked in

● Taking a run-up to an overtake. Drivers of low-powered cars often try this extremely dangerous manoeuvre, which leaves them travelling much faster than the car in front and too close to it. If the car in front brakes, you're in big trouble.

● Being indecisive. Dawdling over an overtake that you should be committed to, is as dangerous as rushing into a manoeuvre. When overtaking, act positively and quickly with excellent observation and anticipation.

● Following another vehicle into an overtake. What if it doesn't pass as quickly as you think or if it has misjudged the overtake altogether. Using other vehicles as a shield, is dangerous and severely limits your view. What if it suddenly pulls in, leaving you to face an oncoming lorry with nowhere to go?

WET WEATHER OVERTAKING

Overtaking in bad weather is more dangerous as visibility can be seriously reduced by spray, and braking distances are significantly increased.

Also remember that, just because you can't see headlights, doesn't mean that there's no vehicle there. Many motorists forget to put their headlights on except when driving at night.

"In a potentially dangerous situation, try to accommodate the driver who's at risk."

Remember, if you're following a lorry and you can't see his mirrors, he can't see you, you're too close and he probably won't even know you're there.

Once the vehicle in front has passed the lorry, proceed with your own overtake. Do it quickly and safely, and be prepared for turbulence as you pass the front of the truck

MAKE OVERTAKING EASIER FOR OTHERS

It can be tempting to challenge a dangerous or poorly-planned overtake, to try to teach the errant driver a lesson. Rise above this novice behaviour and make life as easy as possible for the vulnerable overtaker. You want them as far away from you as possible.

● If you are not intending to overtake, always leave a generous gap in front of you for overtaking vehicles to pull into. Otherwise they may have to attempt a doubly-dangerous two-car overtake.

● Use your mirrors carefully and never compete for an overtaking opportunity with another driver.

● When conditions allow, move slightly to the left to make it easier for others to pass you. Keep your speed constant and, if it won't confuse other road users, give a brief burst of left-hand indication.

● If a dangerous situation occurs during an overtake, try to safely accommodate the errant driver by accelerating or braking to provide them with a safety gap to pull into.

CROSS-HATCHINGS

Cross-hatchings separate potentially dangerous streams of traffic. Advanced Drivers know which ones can and which ones can't be driven on.

Cross-hatchings bound by a solid white line are there to separate carriageways or the approach to a motorway slip road. They should never be driven on, unless there is an emergency or the police direct you to go there.

Cross-hatched areas surrounded by a broken white line are used to separate traffic on some roads, that at some point may have had three lanes. You may enter these areas where you can see it is safe to do so.

These 'hatchings' usually appear on roads with high accident rates. Take extra care when overtaking not to surprise other drivers who are not expecting anyone to drive in this cross-hatched zone.

Refer to the *Highway Code* for more detail.

The unbroken lines surrounding the chevrons cannot be crossed except in an emergency

TWO-WAY ROADS WITH THREE LANES

Britain's dangerous three-lane roads have been much improved in recent years with the addition of cross-hatchings and solid white lines.

Double white lines must never be crossed and keep drivers going in one direction to two lanes and those in the other direction to one lane (there are exceptions to this rule. See the *Highway Code*).

On some roads, particularly on hills, a solid white line is paired with a broken white one. This normally gives the uphill traffic two lanes (so that slow traffic has a 'crawler' lane) and faster downhill traffic just one. However, where the broken white lines are on the side of the single lane, traffic in this lane is allowed to cross the line for an overtake, where it is safe to do so.

While the markings are clearly defined, you should always take care and maintain excellent observation on three lane roads, as other drivers may not have your appreciation of the system.

⚠️ Keep an eye on the people carrier. If you're in his blind-spot, he may inadvertently pull out in front of you.

OVERTAKING AND DUAL CARRIAGEWAYS

Dual carriageways are among Britain's most dangerous roads, because, while the speed limit is the same as a motorway (70mph), there are many more potential hazards to deal with. For example:

- Bicycles, mopeds and tractors can use dual-carriageways.
- There is no hard shoulder for broken down vehicles.
- Side turnings may not have slip-roads.
- Vehicles can emerge from lay-bys.
- Traffic can join or leave the carriageway through the central reservation.
- Pedestrians and dog-walkers are even allowed to cross the carriageways!
- Drivers in the right-hand lane may slow down to turn right across the central reservation.
- Learner drivers can drive at 70mph on dual carriageways.

> "Dual carriageways are among the UK's most dangerous roads, with many unique hazards."

ADVANCED CHECKLIST
- You should always help others to overtake as safely as possible.
- Think about whether you really need to make an overtake.
- Overtaking is invariably a risky manoeuvre.
- Apply the correct overtaking method defined in the 'overtaking triangle'.
- Always plan for the worst.

EXAMINER CHECKLIST
- Are overtaking manoeuvres carried out smoothly, safely and decisively?
- Is the vehicle correctly-positioned throughout?
- Are mirrors, signals and gears used correctly?
- Are speed limits adhered to during an overtake?

Driving in town

Urban driving requires enhanced observation and anticipation. This section will help you perfect your driving talents in town

THE EXTRA DEMANDS OF TOWN DRIVING

Denser traffic and more pedestrians make town and city driving far more intense than driving on the open road. Hazards are also likely to be concealed and there are more junctions and traffic lights etc to deal with. The only way to cope safely with all these potential dangers is to observe and concentrate intensely, spotting them and taking the appropriate measures to avoid them as early as possible.

Local knowledge is particularly useful in town, but you should never let it lure you into a false sense of security, as most accidents occur within five minutes of home, where drivers are most complacent.

Always position your car to achieve the best view ahead, using the information gained to ensure you're in the right lane as early as possible.

Should you make a mistake that cannot easily be rectified with a U-turn, drive on as planned then turn around, making your way back to the correct route.

PLANNING YOUR ROUTE

In a strange town, consult your map or directions when it is safe to do so (in a lay-by or at traffic lights) and make a mental note of the next three or so instructions.

Pull over safely, when you need to check your notes again.

"Most accidents happen within five minutes of home."

ROUTE OBSERVATION IN TOWN

Advanced observation in town helps you to spot many hazards and identify plenty of useful driving information. Here are some important things to look out for...

- Parked cars can obscure hazards. As you pass them, choose a speed and road position that gives you enough reaction time if, for example, a door is opened without warning or someone steps out.
- Spot tell-tale signs that a car is about to pull out: angled wheels, exhaust smoke and illuminated tail-lights etc.
- Look out for pedestrians who are using traffic crossings incorrectly. Many start crossing when the green man 'beeps' without even looking to see if any traffic is approaching. Also keep an eye out for 'late runners', who make a dash for it as your lights turn green
- Be aware of pedestrians near schools and pubs at key times, and near offices, stations etc at all times.
- Give cyclists plenty of clearance as you pass them. Look out for them at junctions and always allow them enough space for a 'wobble'.
- Watch buses and other tall vehicles up ahead. They can give early-warning as to traffic movements.
- Lorries and buses can obscure important road signs. Looking ahead for signs will minimise this problem.

Buses, vans and learner drivers. It's a jungle out there!

- Delivery vans often park in dangerous places, so take extra care when passing them. Remember to look underneath them to spot the feet of pedestrians who may step out into the road unexpectedly.
- Taxis may make unexpected manoeuvres (u-turns, sudden stops) when they spot a fare. Be prepared for this when driving near railway stations and shopping centres etc.

Commentary driving in town (see page 35) really helps to highlight just how much information your brain has to process on any urban drive. Often you'll find you can't verbally describe the changing hazards fast enough! Practise 'describing your drive' whenever possible as it highlights the need for concentration, observation and speed awareness.

LANE DISCIPLINE

Advanced Drivers recognise that lane discipline is crucial in one-way systems to maintain a smooth flow of traffic.

Observe well ahead for turns and exits. This will give you sufficient time to get in the correct lane.

Keep left as much as possible, unless this becomes a 'left-turn only' lane or you need to make a right turn.

Overtaking is allowed in both lanes on a one-way street, but always be aware when 'undertaking', that the vehicle you are passing may not expect to be passed on the inside and may try to pull into your lane. In slow or stationary traffic, also look out for pedestrians crossing and cyclists or motorcyclists who often ignore lane discipline.

ROAD SURFACES IN TOWN

Urban roads can be more slippery than country roads as the coating of oil and rubber on the streets becomes more polished by the constant traffic. Take care, in dry weather, but remember that a light shower (especially on a hot day) is likely to make road surfaces especially hazardous.

Look for oil spills on the road in places where cars stop regularly (junctions, traffic lights etc). Unfortunately, grip is often reduced where it is most essential.

High-friction compounds (like Shell-Grip) are a safety feature applied to road surfaces near hazards and accident blackspots (roundabouts, junctions, traffic lights etc). Be aware that moving from these high-grip compounds to a normal Tarmac surface can

unbalance a car, particularly in the wet, on bends and when travelling too quickly.

Finally, slippery spilled diesel is very common on bends, roundabouts and tight junctions near petrol stations. This is especially dangerous to motorcyclists, so allow them plenty of space.

PARKING

Parking is an essential part of the L-test, so it's amazing how few people do it properly. Scrubbed tyres, kerbed wheels and cars parked on the kerb or sticking into the road are common sights in the UK. Such faults show a lack of ability and/or a complacent attitude.

Novice drivers will often try to drive into a parking space nose-first. Unless the space is very large, this is a mistake and makes it almost impossible to park properly, with your car positioned parallel to the kerb.

Advanced Drivers are expert at parking. They always…
1) Park on the left-hand side of the road, whenever possible.
2) Drive slowly past a potential parking space and size it up to see if their car will fit?
3) Check the road behind is completely clear.
4) Select reverse gear and move backwards in a straight line until the back of their car is level with the back of the parked car.
5) Using left-hand steering lock, they continue reversing

into the space, keeping about one foot (30cm) away from the parked car. When the front of their car has just passed the back of the parked car…
6) …they apply right-hand steering to bring the front of their car into the space and to line the back of their car up with the parked car behind.
7) They reverse right up to the car behind, then pull straight forward, perfecting their position and leaving the vehicles in front and behind enough room to get out.

STOPPING ON HILLS

Don't hold your car on the clutch when you stop on a hill, as it causes overheating and premature wear. Use the handbrake instead, and select neutral if you'll be stopped for more than a few seconds.

When stopping on a hill in traffic, always leave extra space in front to allow for the other car rolling backwards.

CONFIDENCE IN CONGESTED CONDITIONS

City drivers, used to congested conditions, are generally more assertive than those who drive mainly on quiet country roads.

This city driver may appear pushy, but their style is suited to their congested surroundings. It helps avoid jams, and, assuming they know what they are doing and where they are going, their decisive manner shouldn't cause other motorists any problems.

Advanced Drivers are able to adapt their driving to suit their situation. They are as decisive and assertive as conditions require, always aim to make good progress and give themselves space to manoeuvre by positioning their vehicle to create room around them.

ADVANCED CHECKLIST
- Driving in town requires highly-developed selective observation skills to process all the information you'll have to take in.
- Always pull up so that you can see the rear tyres of the car in front on the road.
- Always reverse into parking spaces in one smooth and well-judged manner.
- Anticipation is needed to spot unexpected movements by cyclists, parked vehicles and pedestrians.

EXAMINER CHECKLIST
- Does the driver observe all adverse road surface conditions?
- Are signals, road markings and road signs observed, obeyed and approached correctly?
- The driver avoids blocking other vehicles and causing an obstruction?
- Is the vehicle correctly positioned on the road at all times?
- Is the driving confident and courteous?
- Are all manoeuvres performed competently?

Driving in the countryside

Smooth, sweeping rural roads take some beating when it comes to delivering an enjoyable drive. Use these essential Advanced Driving techniques to develop safe and smooth cross-country roadcraft

OBSERVATION ON THE OPEN ROAD

Driving on country roads requires an entirely different set of skills to driving in congested towns.

Rural roads are arguably the best place to exploit your Advanced Driving abilities and get the most enjoyment out of your driving. Traffic is usually light, you can use your observation skills to safely maintain a higher average speed, the roads are more interesting and you'll have to make well-judged overtakes.

The same level of planning and concentration is required, but you'll be dealing with an entirely different set of hazards and sources of information.

Use all the selective observation skills you have developed, but also consider…
- Taking extra care in case people or vehicles suddenly appear around isolated houses, especially on 60mph roads.
- Looking well ahead (over the hedges, where possible) to spot oncoming traffic in the distance, especially trucks and tractors. Also look for potential overtaking zones and plan your arrival time to coincide with a gap in the oncoming traffic.
- Drains that were once at the side of the road may gradually move further into the road due to erosion of the verges. Hitting these at speed can cause serious damage to cars.
- Livestock in the fields might indicate that there is mud on the road (especially if they are cows that need milking daily. Also, you should always be prepared to encounter a flock of sheep around the next bend.
- The line of hedges, trees or telegraph poles often denotes the direction the road may take around the next bend. Use it to your advantage.
- Holes in hedges are often found on particularly sharp or tightening bends, and are usually created by some unfortunate driver who has overshot the corner and gone straight on. Treat them as a reminder to take care and to keep control of your speed.
- Don't swerve wildly if an animal or bird darts out in front of you. Better a broken foglight or dented bumper than a total loss of control.

Moving out (safely) towards the centre of the road, allows you to take a smoother line through bends

How to be a better driver

SIDE TURNINGS

On fast country roads, even something as simple as a side turning or gateway to a field can become a potential hazard.
When you spot one, always consider reducing your speed, moving your right foot to cover the brake, repositioning you car on the road, then, if a vehicle does appear, observe to see if they have noticed you.
Try to spot side turnings early and take extra care when approaching buildings.

ROAD SURFACES

Rural road surfaces can hold any number of surprises for the unobservant and unwary driver.
Advanced Drivers, on the other hand, are always ready to encounter hazards around the next bend and alter their speed and line accordingly. They are always prepared for...

- loose gravel
- mud
- wet leaves
- potholes
- raised drains
- dead animals
- deep puddles
- extreme cambers
- slippery patches of road
- tightening bends
- fallen branches
- debris from farm machinery

The section of road you can see is clear and dry. But what lies around the bend? Be prepared for the worst

SAFE STOPPING DISTANCES

On a smooth, satisfying, traffic-free drive in the country, it's easy for even the experienced driver to go too fast.

The simple rule you must always apply is: can you stop within the distance you can see to be clear ahead?

Always be prepared for the worst-case scenario, whether that's horse riders, cyclists, oncoming vehicles overtaking a slow-moving tractor and trailer, a broken-down vehicle or even a farmer with his herd of cows.

Always remain a safe stopping distance behind other vehicles and allow extra braking time if someone is driving too close behind you.

If you find yourself following a large van or lorry, drop back a little to gain a better view around them.

Maintain a safe distance between you and the car in front, especially when braking

---

ADVANCED CHECKLIST
- Practise early observation and driving techniques relevant to rural areas.
- Dual-carriageways present many more hazards than motorways.
- Pay attention to the road surface you're driving on.
- Identify hazardous side turnings early and prepare for them.
- Hone your selective observation skills.

EXAMINER CHECKLIST
- Is there evidence of good observation and lateral scanning skills at all times?
- Are all signals, road-markings and signs spotted, obeyed and approached correctly?
- Does the driver observe the road surface, looking out for hazardous conditions?
- Are building lines spotted early and approached with due caution?
- Is the driver's judgement of speed and distance competent when overtaking?
- Is good progress made, taking account of road, traffic and weather conditions?
- Is proper restraint shown in the right places?

5 // ADVANCED MOTORWAY DRIVING

Motorway technique

JOINING A MOTORWAY

Use your off-side wing mirror to help match your speed to that of the traffic in the left-hand lane of the motorway when you join from a slip road. Where necessary, give a right indicator signal. Do it in time to allow for a reaction from drivers on the main carriageway, who may pull into the middle lane, giving you the chance to merge smoothly. Plan your acceleration on the slip road, so that you don't have to brake or accelerate further to join the traffic flow. Constantly use your mirrors to check the main carriageway and other traffic around you, and never commit to changing carriageways without considering a brief glance over your right shoulder.
If you cross over the motorway on a bridge before joining it, take the opportunity to check out the traffic flow below. It allows you to spot severe hold-ups below, giving you the chance to take another route. On the motorway, drive in the left-hand lane until you have adapted to the speed and traffic flow around you.

> ⚠️ **It is dangerous to run out of fuel on a motorway. Do not join a motorway if you think you may not have enough fuel to reach the next petrol station. Stopping your vehicle on a motorway hard-shoulder is extremely hazardous, while driving at 50mph in the slow lane to eke out your last few drops of fuel can be just as risky.**

DIFFICULT APPROACHES

Joining a motorway isn't always straightforward…
● When the motorway slip road rises up to join the main carriageway, your vision and anticipation are limited, so you have less time to judge the traffic flow before merging.
● To minimise this problem, avoid racing other vehicles up the slip road and stay well back from car in front. When following another vehicle, use the two-second rule (Page 89).
● On short slip roads you have to be very decisive. That may mean you need to accelerate very firmly to achieve a safe merging speed in time.
● Some slip roads have cross-hatchings to separate the lanes of traffic. Those bounded by a solid white line can only be entered in an emergency.
● Look well ahead and plan your approach early. Select the lane that allows you to merge most smoothly.
Usually the right-hand lane is the best choice, but occasionally you may want to use the left lane as it merges further up the motorway.

LEAVING A MOTORWAY

Motorway junction signposts are usually positioned one mile and half-a-mile in advance. Use them to plan your exit speed and to select a suitable lane position early.
Junction countdown signs appear 300, 200 and 100 yards before each exit.
Judge your exit speed carefully, especially after driving for long periods at high motorway speeds. Lift your vision up to look further ahead and never be caught out by a short or sharply-curving exit slip road.
Use your mirrors as you leave the motorway, especially if you plan to take the right-hand lane on a multi-lane exit slip road.
On a busy carriageway, it may be worth taking a quick glance over your right shoulder to check for any inconsiderate drivers trying to cut across from the fast lane of the motorway to the exit in one hazardous manoeuvre. This tactic is likely to be carried out at a dangerously high speed.

Check your fuel level, and consider checking the traffic flow on the carriageway before joining a motorway

ADVANCED CHECKLIST

- Observe traffic conditions carefully as you approach a motorway.
- Use you mirrors regularly.
- Double-check your blind spots.
- Match your speed to the traffic flow in the left-hand lane when joining a motorway.
- Maintain excellent lane discipline.
- Watch your speed when leaving a motorway and at the end of the exit slip road.
- Plan your exit from the motorway in good time.

EXAMINER CHECKLIST

- Is proper use made of mirrors?
- Is an understanding of positioning and traffic flow displayed?
- Is good judgement displayed when joining a motorway?
- Is acceleration sense used on the slip road, to join with traffic in the left-hand lane?
- Is the left-hand lane used in plenty of time when exiting a motorway?

NOTE: Not all test routes will feature motorway evaluation.

On the motorway

Make good, safe progress on all Britain's motorways with these simple Advanced Driving skills. This section tells you how to stay stress-free and silky-smooth from a jam-packed M25 to an empty M6

CONCENTRATION AND OBSERVATION

The lack of stimuli when driving on motorways means that it takes extra concentration to stay alert and observant. Yes, motorways can be boring. You don't have to accelerate, change gear or brake much, the view is often unchanging and there's relatively little steering input needed. It's very easy for your mind to wander in these conditions.

As Advanced Driving is more mentally challenging than standard driving, it keeps you alert. Motorway driving suddenly becomes like a mobile, high-stakes game of chess. You have to plan a route, anticipate traffic movement and be ultra-observant while constantly checking speeds and distances in front and behind your vehicle.

Advanced Drivers do all this while driving smoothly, safely and progressively.

LANE DISCIPLINE

Advanced Drivers have excellent lane discipline and are always in the correct lane for their speed and planned route.

They constantly observe the behaviour of vehicles around them, including regular checking of their mirrors.

As an Advanced Driver you stay in the left-hand lane wherever possible, but don't get so hung up on this that you're constantly diving in and out of the slow lane.

Drivers on UK motorways often display poor lane discipline. This causes frustration and problems for other drivers and can even lead to crashes. You'll often

find traffic gravitating into the right-hand overtaking lane to avoid day-dreamers in the middle lane.

Inconsiderate drivers blocking the middle lane of the motorway are a common problem. Never be tempted to teach them a lesson. Do not flash your lights or sound the horn. Simply overtake them as safely and as soon as you can.

SPEED

Driving faster than 70mph on UK motorways is illegal.

Advanced Drivers travel at an appropriate speed for the road conditions. However, it's easy for your speed to creep up in a modern car, so check your speedometer regularly or use your cruise control.

Motorways are the UK's safest roads, but they are still the scene of numerous incidents and many are policed by speed regulation devices designed to maintain safety.

KEEPING YOUR DISTANCE

At 70mph on a dry motorway, it takes an alert driver over 20 metres to react to a hazard, and – if he's driving a new, performance car on new tyres – at least 50 metres* to stop. That's a minimum of 70 metres covered between spotting a hazard and stopping the vehicle. (A distance equivalent to 14 people carriers!)

This demonstrates what utter lunacy it is when most drivers follow other vehicles at a distance of four or five metres.

Keeping your distance not only increases your view around the car in front, it gives you extra thinking and braking time. Advanced Drivers obey the two-second rule – they stay at least two seconds behind the car in front. Better still, if

you're happy with your cruising speed, stay 100m behind the car in front. This distance is easy to judge, as the white motorway marker posts are positioned 100 metres apart.

Tailgating is extremely common on Britain's busy roads, but you should never get wound up by this ridiculous and dangerous driving style – instead let tailgaters pass as soon as you can.

If a particularly absent-minded and persistent tailgater is proving to be a distraction, don't be intimidated, just look for the first opportunity to move out of the way and consider slowing down and moving into the left-hand lane to encourage him to pass.

On Britain's busy motorways

it can seem almost impossible to maintain a safe (two-second) following distance. Leave a space that big and novice drivers will unwittingly try to fill it. Many will even undertake you and pull-in in front. Despite this, you should always endeavour to keep a safe distance, of at least two seconds, behind the car ahead.

Advanced Drivers always brake in a way that doesn't surprise the car behind them. Usually, that driver won't be adhering to the two-second rule. To protect him, aim to spot hazards early, and in urgent situations, consider using your hazard warning lights to highlight the danger to following drivers.

Test data from Goodyear Tyre Co.

SLIP ROAD COURTESY

As you approach and pass an entrance slip road leading to your carriageway, observe the flow of traffic on it, and consider whether you should

move into the right-hand lane to help the vehicles merge and to avoid being impeded.

Lorry drivers will be very appreciative of your courtesy,

as they are less able to vary their speed to match the traffic flow. If they are forced to slow right down they become a mobile motorway hazard.

CHANGING LANES AND OVERTAKING

Use your mirrors with care when overtaking on a motorway. When required, signal early, giving other road users time to react – many will happily accommodate your manoeuvre. Change lanes gradually and never expect or force other drivers to move out of your way.

Acceleration may sometimes be necessary, but never get in the way of faster vehicles.

In heavy traffic, use the signal as a request, before you plan to change lanes. It is a matter of courtesy and allows following drivers to accommodate your intended manoeuvre. Finally, adjust your speed so that it matches the traffic flow in the faster or slower lane.

Don't compromise your safe following distance (or that of the car behind you) when changing lanes, and always look out for other cars aiming to pull into the same space as you from another lane.

Your indicator signals should only be used to inform others of what you intend to do, not to order them to get out of the way. Watch out for drivers who try to dictate to other road users by leaving their indicators on for prolonged periods.

Drive courteously and in a planned way. Where safe, accommodate other drivers by changing lanes to allow them in or by slowing/accelerating to create a safe gap.

Only use your signals when someone will benefit from the information, and always check your blind spots before making your manoeuvre.

In congested traffic, if your lane is moving faster you may pass traffic on your right. Don't use this as an excuse for blatant 'undertaking', and avoid lane hopping.

MOTORWAY WARNING SIGNALS

Motorway roadside and gantry warning signs advise drivers of dangers ahead, speed limits and carriageway closures. Make sure you are familiar with all the signs in the *Highway Code* and always obey the instruction, even if a problem isn't immediately obvious.

Matrix signs give detailed information and are often used on busy motorways to impose temporary speed limits at rush hour. This slows traffic to keep it flowing, avoiding the frustrating and dangerous stop/starting common to many of the UK's motorways.

> "The nearest emergency phone on a motorway is marked on a post, and never more than half-a-mile away."

TRAFFIC INFORMATION

Plan your long journeys carefully to avoid hold-ups and hazards. In-depth travel information is available on websites (AA/RAC/Highways Agency), via satellite navigation systems, through your mobile phone and on radio stations (local stations and Radio Five Live are good). During your journey, stay up-to-date by pressing the traffic announcement button (TA/TP) on your car radio for regular reports on roads in the region you're travelling through.

COMBAT FATIGUE

Motorways are fast, safe and boring. The monotony of driving long distances, cocooned in a warm car with very little driving input (automatic gearboxes, cruise control, power steering and even auto lights and wipers do all the work for you!) can lead to complacency and fatigue. To counter this effect…

- Consider taking an alternative, more interesting route, perhaps on an A or B-Road. Check your map for parallel routes or set your Sat Nav to avoid motorways.
- Open a window. Cold air will liven you up for a brief period.
- Turn the air-conditioning to cold and direct a vent onto your face.
- Disengage your cruise control.
- Put the radio on or start a conversation with your passenger.
- Stop for a tea, coffee or caffeine drink as soon as is safely possible. Do this every two hours, to maintain your concentration.

Think passenger safety when broken down. High-visibility jackets can be good for your health!

THE MOTORWAY HARD SHOULDER

Many motorway breakdowns would be avoided if drivers took better care of their vehicles – especially the tyres, oil, coolant and fuel levels.

The hard shoulder is an extremely hazardous place to be. To minimise the danger, pull over to the far-left side, put your hazard warning lights on, turn your steered wheels to the left, then get all the passengers out of the car via the near-side doors and move them onto the verge behind the barrier (and to the rear of the car to avoid any flying debris, if passing traffic

strikes your vehicle). Stay near your vehicle or find the nearest emergency phone (the direction of which is marked by arrows on a marker post and is never more than half-a-mile away).

If possible, wear reflective or high-visibility clothing to increase the chances of other motorists spotting you.

On rejoining the motorway, use the hard shoulder as an acceleration lane, to match your speed to the flow of the traffic. Avoid any debris (delaminated tyre tread or exhausts) in your path.

ADVANCED CHECKLIST
- Position your vehicle safely behind the car in front, using the two-second rule.
- 70mph is the limit, not a target speed.
- Practise lane discipline.
- Do not let your driving skills or concentration lapse on long, boring journeys.
- Use advanced observation, anticipation and courtesy to merge smoothly when changing lanes.

EXAMINER CHECKLIST
- Are speed limits observed?
- Is a safe following distance maintained?
- Is the use of mirrors, signalling and lane discipline of a high standard?
- Are speed, distance and other traffic movements judged competently?

6 // ADVANCED DRIVING IN DIFFICULT CONDITIONS

Driving on motorways in bad weather

Britain's notorious weather can cause major problems on any road, and busy motorways are no exception

DRIVING IN HEAVY RAIN

• Motorway spray, caused by heavy rain, can cut visibility to zero. Lorries blast up an almost impenetrable wall of water that fills the air, coats your windscreen and wipes out your view totally for vital seconds. Plan wet-weather motorway overtakes carefully. Hang further back out of the spray and observe the road and traffic ahead. When conditions are most suitable (the route ahead is clear and straight), put your wipers on their fastest setting and move safely, quickly and decisively past the lorry.

With good planning your view should be impeded for only a fraction of a second at worst.
• Heavy rain creates pools of water across the carriageway which can cause a car to aquaplane. This is where the car skims across the surface of the water and has no contact with the road surface. Aquaplaning affects your control by reducing the effect of steering and braking inputs. If you see water pooling or streaming across the road, do not brake or accelerate, instead ease off the accelerator, grip

the steering wheel firmly and try to steer straight ahead. Standing water will pull on the steering wheel and you may need to make corrective inputs when you hit Tarmac again.
• Disengage cruise control.
• On hills, diagonal streams of water often cascade across the carriageway. Be extra vigilant and slow down gradually in very wet conditions.
• Braking distances increase hugely in the rain. Compensate by slowing down, looking further ahead and increasing your following distance.

FOG

• Avoid driving in fog whenever possible.
• Most motorists drive far too fast and much too close together in foggy conditions.
• As always, ensure you can

stop safely within the distance you can see clearly. Constantly ask yourself, if the next thing you saw in front of you was a stationary vehicle involved in an accident, would you be able to

stop in time?
• Keep to the left-hand or centre lane.
• Drive on dipped headlights and put your fog lights on.
• Don't take any chances.

STRONG WINDS

• Strong cross-winds and turbulence can severely unsettle your car and even change your direction of travel.
• Prepare for strong, unsettling winds when you drive on to a flyover or viaduct, where protective embankments disappear. Driving past HGVs at

speed, has a similar effect.
• Be aware of the effects of strong winds on motorcycles and other vehicles like high-sided lorries, vans and caravans. Give them a wide berth, plan your overtake away from the high-risk locations mentioned previously and

consider leaving the middle lane as a 'buffer zone'.
• Take extra care when driving flat-sided vehicles like vans, people carriers and 4x4s. Grip the steering wheel firmly and be ready to counter the unsettling 'deflection' when you pass an HGV.

ICE AND SNOW

- Avoid driving in extremely wintry conditions. Is any journey really worth the risk?
- Only in extreme cases, are motorways affected by settling snow. Usually snowploughs and gritter lorries keep them clear. However, slip roads and hard shoulders don't always get the same treatment, so take extra care.
Also be aware that bridges are particularly susceptible to re-freezing and black ice.

- In sub-zero conditions, drive at a safe speed, allow extra braking distance and make extra-smooth steering and braking inputs to avoid unsettling your vehicle.
- If you have to travel in extreme conditions, ensure you have plenty of fuel, take a shovel, spare warm clothes and other essential supplies like water to drink.
- In extreme winter conditions, drive as if you are walking on

eggs! Stay in a high gear and don't make any sudden inputs as these may cause a slide.
- The left-hand lane carries most traffic, so is likely to be the most clear of snow and ice. Stay there as much as possible.
- Do not put your wheels on, or try to drive through the lines of slush and ice that collect between lanes.
(For more tips on general driving in ice and snow see page 98.)

HEADLIGHTS AND FOGLIGHTS

- When changing lanes in poor weather, look extra carefully in your mirrors for vehicles travelling without lights on.
- As soon as conditions clear, remember to turn your foglights off. It is an offence to leave them on in good visibility or at night when your headlights would be adequate.
- Avoid over-use of foglights/driving lights. Their high-intensity beams may blind other road users in clear conditions.
- Only use rear foglights in extreme conditions as they can be dazzling and annoying. They might also mask the fact that

your brake lights have come on.
- Be aware that foglights cancel when full-beam is used.
(For more tips on general driving in fog see page 97.)

Advanced driving in tricky conditions

Advanced Drivers are equipped to drive with skill and precision in any conditions, day or night, and whatever the weather. Our tips will make you a confident driver, 24/7

DRIVING AT NIGHT

The fundamental rule of Advanced Driving – you must be able to stop within the distance you can see to be clear – is especially important when driving at night.

Away from street lighting, your vision will be limited to the range of your headlights, and this varies massively between dipped and full-beam. Therefore, it makes sense that you slow down when you're driving on dipped headlights.

If you find your speed creeping up, remind yourself how dangerous it would be if you suddenly came across another car, a tyre carcass, a pedestrian or even a stray animal in your headlight beam!

If your headlights illuminate 40 metres ahead, you'll have just 1.5 seconds to react and stop at 60mph! Realistically, you'll still be travelling at around 40mph when you hit the obstruction!!

Drive on full-beam whenever possible, but always think about other road users. Dip your lights as late as you possibly can, ensuring that you do not dazzle anyone, and remembering that, at night, your lights give other road-users the earliest warning of your presence.

Clean your lights regularly, as road grime quickly reduces their effectiveness, and the distance you can see ahead clearly.

THE BENEFITS OF NIGHT DRIVING

Advanced Drivers know that driving in the dark isn't all danger and drawbacks. Empty night-time roads make journeys quicker and less stressful; car headlights give early warning of their presence, and the skilled driver can even use other vehicles' headlight beams to work out where the road goes next.

Don't be complacent though, speed is more difficult to judge in the dark – especially approach speeds – so you should still take care and adhere to all the daylight driving rules.

CHECKING YOUR LIGHTS

Regularly check that your lights work properly. While someone observes the lights outside the car, run through all the switches: headlights (full and dipped), sidelights, foglights, indicators, brake lights, reverse lights, hazard-warning lights and even number plate lights and door courtesy lights.

If alone, park your vehicle in front of your garage door. Illuminate all your lights in sequence and look for the reflections off the door to make sure all the bulbs are working.

"Speed is more difficult to judge in the dark – especially approach speed."

DAZZLE

If an approaching car forgets to dip, glance immediately towards the side of the road to avoid being temporarily blinded. On a dual-carriageway at 70mph you cover 31 metres (about seven car lengths) per second, so even if it takes only five seconds for your vision to clear fully, you'll have covered a distance equivalent to one and a half football pitches! With practice, this avoidance technique becomes habit.

Give the offending driver a brief flash to remind him he's on full-beam, but never stay on full-beam yourself to retaliate.

Dazzle from following vehicles is just as blinding, but the effect can usually be 'minimised' using the dipping interior mirror which is now standard on most vehicles. Don't forget to return the mirror to its 'normal position' once the dazzle has subsided.

Only use your fog lights when visibility is less than 100 metres

ADVANCED CHECKLIST

- Be aware that it's more difficult to judge distance and speed in the dark.
- Ensure you can always stop safely within the distance you can clearly see in your headlight beam.
- Maintain and clean all your lights regularly.
- Select dipped and mainbeam lights with consideration for others and the driving conditions.
- Carry spare bulbs in case one of your lights fails at night (This is the law in continental Europe).
- Stop for regular breaks when making long journeys, especially at night.
- Tiredness is a killer. It affects reaction times and concentration.

EYESIGHT AND FATIGUE

Many eyesight problems are enhanced when driving at twilight or in the dark. A dirty windscreen can also impair a driver's vision.

Driving long distances in the dark is very tiring on the eyes, as they have to constantly adjust and work much harder than in the daytime.

Every year, a significant number of car crashes are caused by drivers falling asleep at the wheel. Don't become a statistic. Whenever possible, avoid making long journeys after a full day at work, have a light snack (not a heavy meal) before setting off and avoid alcohol or drugs.

If you start to feel tired whilst driving, a blast of cool air from the air-conditioning or an open window will only perk you up briefly, until you find a safe place to stop.

Take a break at least every two hours. Once you're stopped, get out of the car, have a good stretch and then try to rest your eyes. Drink a cup of tea or coffee or have a high-caffeine 'energy' drink. Seriously consider taking a quick nap ('power-napping' is proven to significantly increase awareness) and only get back behind the wheel when you feel properly refreshed.

Always try to avoid driving between the hours of 12am and 6am as the effects of tiredness are most pronounced between these times.

DRIVING IN FOG

Advanced Drivers always drive within the limits of what they can see. This is especially important in foggy conditions as the lack of vision seriously affects your sense of speed and distance.

Do your best to avoid travelling in thick fog as it is one of the most dangerous driving conditions you'll encounter. If you *have* to drive, you should only travel at very low speeds. That said, even this this can put you at danger from reckless drivers who refuse to slow down and gamble their lives and those of other road users. Minimise the dangers by following these rules…

- As soon as you see fog developing, slow down and switch on your headlights.
- Fog density can change in a matter of a few metres. You can go from a light mist to a pea-souper in a second. Ensure you drive accordingly.
- Use windscreen wipers on the intermittent setting to clear the fine mist of moisture that collects on your windscreen.
- The strain of peering through thick fog quickly makes you tired. Take regular breaks.
- Take extreme care as you accelerate in preparation for any overtaking manoeuvre.
- Never go ahead with a manoeuvre based on the fact that you can't see any lights. Not everyone will remember to put their lights on.
- Never be pressured into driving faster than you feel is safe by tailgaters.
- Likewise, don't drive faster than you feel comfortable with, just to keep up with the rear lights of the car in front.

- Use front and rear foglights when visibility is down to 100 metres or less.
- Avoid using mainbeams in fog. The bright illumination reflects off the fog, impairing your view by creating a 'wall of white' in front of you. Use dipped lights and consider using low-mounted front foglights which will help you to pick out the road markings or the verge at the edge of the road. High-powered rear foglights should only be switched on in thick fog.
- Remember to turn off your foglights when the fog clears.
- When turning right in fog, flash your lights and sound your horn to warn any oncoming traffic hidden in the fog. Move as quickly as you safely can across the other carriageway.
- Fog can suddenly appear in dense patches. It generally occurs first (and is usually thicker) near water eg: on coastal roads, bridges, near ponds, rivers and lakes.

"When driving, tiredness can be a killer, as it affects reaction times and concentration."

ADVANCED CHECKLIST
- **Postpone a journey if conditions are very bad.**
- **Slow down in fog, so that you can stop within the distance you can see to be clear ahead.**
- **For the best visibility in fog use dipped lights and foglights, not main beam.**
- **Avoid overtaking or trying to stay in touch with a car that you think is travelling too fast.**
- **Allow enough space in front, so that you could pull up in time if the car ahead were to stop dead in a collision.**
- **Remember fog makes the road damp and covers your windscreen with moisture that can impair your vision further.**
- **Do you drive at an appropriate speed when visibility is reduced?**
- **Do you drive a safe distance behind vehicles in front of you?**

DRIVING IN WINTER

Freezing weather creates many new hazards, from poor visibility to a dangerous lack of grip. Try to avoid driving in these conditions, but if you have to get behind the wheel, you'll need extra concentration, anticipation and the following techniques to negotiate these hazards safely.

DRIVING IN ICE AND SNOW

- Every autumn, prepare your vehicle for winter. Have your antifreeze checked, replace damaged wiper blades, stock-up on de-icer and screenwash and buy a window scraper and two cloths: one to clear condensation off the inside of your windscreen and one to clean lights and exterior glass. Drivers of older cars may also consider buying a can of moisture-dispersant like WD40. This is designed to keep spark plugs and distributors functioning properly.
- Many new cars have built-in external temperature gauges. Use them as an early-warning system to assess driving conditions. An indicated temperature of 3°C or below, means that extremely slippery conditions are possible.
- Adjust your driving to the constantly-changing conditions. Always drive within your own – and your car's – limits.
- Observe other road users to see how they react to the conditions ahead. Alter your driving style accordingly.
- Stopping distances can increase dramatically in winter. Stay focused; look further ahead for potential hazards and ensure that you are far enough behind the car in front, to stop comfortably if it brakes.
- Driving long distances in bad weather can be tiring. Poor visibility and the mesmeric effect of windscreen wipers can take their toll. Stop for a break at least every two hours.
- In low-traction conditions, stay in the highest gear possible, as it minimises wheelspin. Consider setting off in second gear, releasing the clutch and accelerating gently.
- Always aim to stay on snow-ploughed and gritted carriageways. Overtaking manoeuvres on a snowy fast-lane are incredibly dangerous.
- If a driver tailgates you in wintry conditions, be prepared to pull over and let him pass. You may also consider helping him out of the hedge, some way down the road.
- In freezing conditions, Advanced Drivers make an effort to drive more smoothly than ever. Clutch, acceleration and steering movements should be smooth and progressive and braking should be done early and gently.
- Modern ABS systems can make a horrible 'graunching' sound when you brake on ice or snow. This is because they are repeatedly applying the brakes (many hundreds of times a second) in an effort to prevent a skid. This sound is quite normal and not a cause for concern, as long as it stops when the brake is released and the car brakes normally when back on a grippy surface. If the noise persists, stop as soon as possible and have your brakes checked by a mechanic.
- Bridges are particularly prone to icing up. They freeze first, thaw last and are often lined with concrete pillars that don't mix well with vehicle paint and bodywork!
- The worst freezing usually takes place at night and in the early hours. Avoid driving at these times if possible.
- The grooved finish on concrete road surfaces often collects water, which freezes in winter making them particularly hazardous.
- Be aware that even as snow melts, and other drivers' confidence returns, the conditions can remain extremely hazardous.
- Even after any snow or frost has gone, ice can remain in areas shaded by trees and buildings. Be aware when crossing shady sections of road that your vehicle's grip may be significantly reduced, especially on bends.
- Black ice is almost invisible and it reduces a car's grip to zero. If you hit black ice, there

is little you can do to control a car. However, as it usually appears in patches, you should be prepared for the moment when your car regains its grip.

• If your car loses grip at the front end, a front-wheel skid (understeer) will begin. Take your foot off the accelerator, consider disengaging the clutch and steer smoothly. If your car has traction control, you may not need to declutch.
When the tyres bite again, steer the car back on course.

• If your car goes into a rear-wheel skid, the tail of the car will swing out sideways (oversteer) and may cause a spin if you don't correct it quickly enough. To control the skid, lift off the accelerator, consider de-clutching and steer

in the direction of the skid – so that the front wheels continue to point in the direction you intend to travel. This technique is called opposite lock – it requires quick reactions, a cool head and a smooth response. Many drivers will find this reaction to a skid instinctive, but most will also over-correct and end up out of control, fishtailing down the road.

• Always make sure your windows, lights and mirrors are clear of dirt and ice before setting off on a journey.

• Take care if you leave your car unattended with the engine running to warm up.
If someone steals it with the keys left inside, you may find that your insurer will not pay out.

"Many drivers will react to a skid instinctively. But most will over-correct and end up fishtailing down the road."

DRIVING IN SUMMER

Road surfaces can become very slippery in summer, especially after rain or a heavy dew. Debris particles (dust, rubber and oil etc) can also build up on the road surface, severely reducing grip levels. Tarmac also becomes slippery when it gets 'polished' after a long dry spell.

Here are more Advanced Driving tips for summer…
- Summer storms can create flash floods in minutes. Excess rain water takes the line of least resistance, which often means flowing down or across a road. If this happens, slow down to an appropriate speed, keep a careful eye on the depth of the water and prepare yourself for reduced visibility and grip. Always try your brakes immediately after driving through large puddles or floods.
- Never try to drive through deep water at speed. Just 10mm of water can make a car aquaplane, taking control from the driver for vital seconds. Deeper water will pull on the steering wheel violently. It can cause an instant change of direction or even a spin.
- If you think a pool or flood might be too deep for your car to drive through, look for evidence of the water depth (relative to kerbstones or verges perhaps). By the time you have

checked, a novice driver may have taken the 'plunge' first.
- Drive through floods slowly and smoothly in first gear. (Keep your revs high, slipping the clutch in a manual car. In an automatic, left-foot brake while keeping the revs high with the right foot.)
- Never enter floods that would immerse your car's air intake or sparkplugs (approximately halfway between the top of the wheel arch and the top of the bonnet). Your car will stop instantly leaving you stranded, and potentially with damage to your engine. (Check the manufacturer's handbook.)
- Don't enter a flood when there is traffic coming in the opposite direction. Their 'bow-wave' could cause your engine to become flooded.
- Worn road surfaces are often resurfaced with loose stone chippings in summer. Take care not to skid on them when they are first laid, especially where they 'pool' on

bends and at the road's edges. Also, hang well back from the car ahead to avoid your car getting pebble-dashed.
- Holiday drivers often present more of a risk than ordinary drivers. They may be relaxed to the point of complacency or stressed and distracted by their kids. They are usually driving on strange roads and may be tired after a long journey.
- Maintain excellent visibility by keeping your windscreen and lights clear of dead bugs and splashes of tar. While you may have reasonable vision in the dry, the minute it rains or becomes dark, your view may well be dangerously limited.

ADVANCED CHECKLIST
- **Prepare your car for winter every autumn.**
- **Use your car's controls more smoothly when driving in wintry conditions to avoid skidding.**
- **Always be prepared for slippery spots by reading the road ahead. Look for shady areas, bridges and places where water might have gathered.**
- **Familiarise yourself with the techniques for controlling front and rear-end skids. Consider taking a skidpan course.**
- **When stuck in snow, use the highest-possible gear and gentle throttle to avoid wheelspin.**

EXAMINER CHECKLIST
- **Is the road surface observed carefully, especially in bad weather?**
- **Does the car appear to be well maintained?**
- **Is the vehicle driven with restraint and with extra sensitivity when roads are slippery?**
- **Is the driver aware of extended braking distances and the need for enhanced acceleration sense in slippery conditions?**
- **Are the vehicle's windscreen and lights clean?**

Roadworks and breakdowns

From motorways to C-roads, the UK's highways are plagued with roadworks. Here we show you how to handle them efficiently and safely

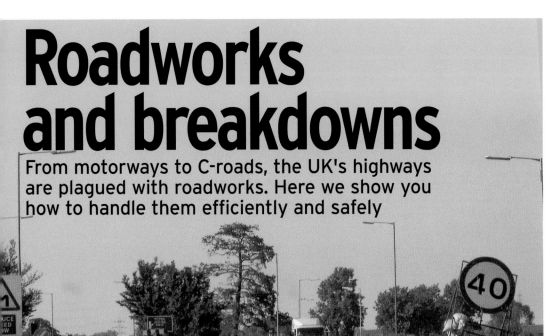

ROADWORKS AND CONTRAFLOWS

A sophisticated system of warning signs and coning has been developed to keep traffic as safe and mobile as possible through roadworks and contraflows. Special care must be taken when negotiating these hazards.

● Change lanes in good time, using excellent observation and clear signalling.

● Forcing your way in just before the carriageway narrows, causes a chain of braking that makes traffic further back come to a complete standstill

● 'Zip' merging – where each car lets one other car in – is a more effective way of keeping the traffic moving.

● Where possible, stay in the safer left-hand lane in contraflows. Changing carriageways, and driving next to motorway traffic in narrow lanes separated only by a line of plastic cones, increases the risk of an accident.

● Be extra vigilant about speed limits through roadworks, as speed cameras are often positioned here. It's all too easy to break a 40mph limit on a quiet road in a modern car.

● Keep an eye out for debris like exhaust pipes and tyre carcasses on the carriageway, especially on narrow, restricted lanes and the hard shoulder.

ADVANCED CHECKLIST

● Take notice of and obey all motorway warning signs.

● Choose your lane early when approaching roadworks.

● Avoid crossing the central reservation into the contraflow lane as it is more dangerous than staying on your own carriageway.

● Take extreme safety measures if you have to stop on the hard shoulder.

● Use the hard shoulder as an acceleration lane when rejoining the motorway.

7 // ESSENTIAL KNOWLEDGE

First aid, emergencies and personal safety

Most drivers encounter or are involved in a car crash during their driving careers. How they react can mean the difference between life and death

ACCIDENTS

Avoid becoming an 'accidental pedestrian', vulnerable to danger, when you exit your vehicle at the roadside. Consider all the dangers posed by passing traffic, and act accordingly.
1) Carry high-visibility jackets for you and your passengers.
2) Ensure that everyone involved is out of immediate danger, then protect the crash site from further accidents, using a warning triangle (unless on a motorway) and your hazard-warning lights.
3) Don't park your vehicle where it may be a hazard to other traffic or where it blocks emergency vehicle access. In the dark, try to park your car so that its headlights illuminate the accident scene.
4) Call 999 (112 on a mobile phone) for help. Give your precise location, and tell them: how many casualties there are; how serious any injuries are; how many (and what kind of) vehicles are involved in the crash and if there are any fuel or chemical spillages.

5) The first minutes after an accident are crucial to the well-being of any casualties. Do whatever you can to help, even if it is just offering support and encouragement.
6) Do not move any incapacitated casualties, or the vehicle they are in, unless there is an imminent risk of fire.
7) Switch off the engines of all vehicles involved and apply their handbrakes if possible.
8) Make sure nobody in the vicinity smokes.

9) Approaching vehicles need as much notice as possible of the accident. Walk back up the side of the road at least 100 metres, facing the oncoming traffic flow, giving a clear 'slow down' signal and pointing to where the accident is. Do not stand in the road.
10) Allocate someone to direct vehicles around the accident. Make sure they are clearly visible by positioning them in the headlamp beam of a stationary car.

HELPING CASUALTIES

- Only move casualties if they are in immediate danger, as it could aggravate their injuries, causing paralysis or even death.
- Ensure that they are breathing. Remove food or chewing gum from their mouth, loosen their collar and undo helmet straps, leaving the helmet on.
- If you can't detect breathing, consider mouth-to-mouth resuscitation. To do this, place the casualty on their back. Support the neck so that the head falls backwards, opening the airway. Pinch their nose and hold their mouth open. Cover their mouth with yours and blow firmly to inflate the lungs. Then release the mouth and nose.
- Check for breathing. If it is not apparent, repeat the procedure above until the casualty starts to breathe.
- If the casualty is unconscious, place them in the recovery position, on their side with an arm and leg positioned to keep them there. Turn their head so that it is facing slightly downwards to prevent choking.
- If the casualty is bleeding, apply firm pressure to the wound. If you have a First Aid kit, bandage a sterile dressing firmly over the wound.

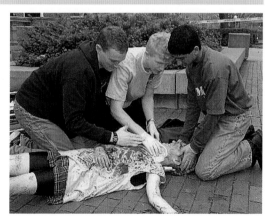

- Prevent fracture injuries from being moved.
- If the casualty is conscious, sitting up in the car and in no immediate danger – do not move them. Support their head in case they pass out.
- Keep all casualties warm, especially those in shock. Do not give them alcohol, drugs, food, drinks or cigarettes. These may aggravate any internal injuries.
- This is basic First Aid advice. For more details log on to: www.redcross.org.uk.

REMOVING AN INJURED MOTORCYCLIST'S HELMET

In consultation with experts, the IAM has created these 'helmet-removal' guidelines:

• If the motorcyclist is breathing and there is no danger of choking, leave the helmet on, but open the visor.

• If the rider is unconscious or has stopped breathing, you have less than four minutes to act to prevent irreparable brain damage or death.

• Open the visor and unfasten the chinstrap.

• It takes two people to remove a helmet safely.

• One supports the head and neck, the other lifts the helmet.

• Lift the helmet backwards off the chin first, then away from the base of the skull.

• Continue to support the head and neck until a surgical collar is fitted.

TRAVELLING ALONE

Let people know where you are going and when you're hoping to arrive. Take a mobile phone and keep the car doors locked. In the event of a breakdown, stay in your car.

If you are a woman travelling alone, let the recovery services and the Highways Agency know, as you should receive priority treatment.

Keep valuables secure and out of sight. Pre-program your mobile phone with emergency contact numbers.

If you suspect a following vehicle is anything more than just an inconsiderate driver, drive to the nearest police station or public place before stopping. If stopped by the police, ask to see identification before unlocking the doors or opening the windows. If in doubt call 999 or 112.

Finally, always lock your car after refuelling and take your bag with you.

WHAT TO DO IN THE EVENT OF AN ACCIDENT

Never drive away from the scene of an accident you're involved in, without first speaking to the other people involved or leaving your contact details. Also, remember to remove the keys from the ignition, even if you leave your car for just a moment.

• At any accident, give your name, address, registration and insurance company details to the other parties involved. It is your responsibility to get the same details from other drivers.

• Uninsured and unregistered drivers are common on the UK's roads. If you're suspicious that the other driver may not be driving legally, contact the police straight away. If they don't want you to call the police, quickly have a look at their tax disc. If this is out of date, other essentials like MOT and insurance may be too.

• In minor incidents, drivers often want to pay for repairs themselves, rather than affect their no-claims bonus. If this is the case, don't let them leave the scene until you have their name and address and have seen some proof of ID.

• Get details of any witnesses. Do this quickly, as they often disappear once everything is under control.

• You do not have to involve the police, but it is best to do so if anyone is injured or there are allegations of dangerous or illegal driving. If you call for an ambulance or the fire brigade the police should arrive automatically.

• Even if you only tap or scrape another car in a car park, you are required by law to leave your contact details.

• In a serious accident, don't move any vehicles until the police arrive. If you have a camera on your phone, take pictures and video of the scene, as this evidence will be useful should a court case be needed. Also, consider taking notes and measurements, if you think the information might be useful for the police or your insurance company.

• Insurers advise that you leave the assessment of blame to them and the police, so avoid admitting liability at the scene of the accident.

• Try not to get emotional and angry if someone crashes into you. Stay calm, swap details as quickly as possible, then clear the road to prevent delay to other drivers.

• If you witness a hit and run incident, write down as many details as possible about it: car make, model and registration number, car colour, what happened, driver description etc. Remember though, the victim should always be your first priority.

• Finally, don't 'rubberneck' when passing the scene of a crash... this invariably causes delays and can even lead to other accidents.

FIRST AID KITS

Carrying a First Aid kit in your car, could save a life one day. Many new cars feature them as standard, but they're also available to buy from stores like Halford's or Boots.

Ensure your kit is up-to-date and contains: plasters, surgical dressings, bandages, slings, safety pins, scissors and a knife.

Never offer a casualty any type of medication or drug, as you may leave yourself open to being sued if anything should go wrong.

Another useful precaution is to input an I.C.E (**I**n **C**ase of **E**mergency) number into your mobile phone. Emergency services use this to quickly contact next of kin in the event of an accident.

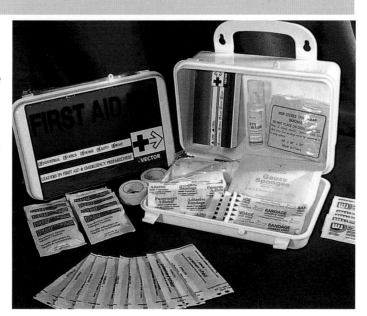

Opening a car's bonnet feeds oxygen to a burning engine, fanning the flames

"If you use a fire extinguisher, aim it at the base of the fire and keep it there until the fire is completely out."

FIRE

Fire, or the imminent risk of fire, is one of the few reasons you should ever pull an injured person from a car.

At any crash scene, quickly check for leaking fuel. If you find it, or there is a strong smell of fumes, isolate the area, keeping anyone who isn't essential to proceedings well clear. Shorting wires or even static electricity could cause a spark, so take care. Always turn off the ignition and, if there is a sparking cable or wire, consider disconnecting the car's battery.

If you suspect an engine fire, never open the bonnet, as this will feed oxygen to the flames.

If you carry a fire extinguisher in your car, aim it at the base of the flames and keep it there until the fire is completely out.

A vehicle fire extinguisher makes a great investment and should be considered by any motorist. They are relatively inexpensive and are available from most motoring stores.

ADVANCED CHECKLIST

- Carry a reflective jacket.
- At the scene of an accident, act quickly and decisively.
- Carry a First Aid kit and know how to use it.
- Consider carrying a fire extinguisher.
- Use your phone's camera to take pictures or to record video evidence at the scene.
- In minor accidents where no-one is injured, swap information (name, contact and insurance company details). Do not admit liability and clear the road as quickly as possible.

Driving abroad

HINTS AND TIPS

Most foreign countries drive on the right-hand side of the road. This requires extra concentration, awareness and observation for anyone used to driving on the left. These tips will help you to maintain high driving standards, everywhere from Azerbijan (right-hand driving) to Zimbabwe (left-hand driving).

- Maintain your concentration levels at all times. Loss of focus could mean you unintentionally turn into an oncoming lane of traffic at a junction.
- Every time you start your car, remind yourself where you are driving. This is especially important when there's not much traffic around.
- Finding it difficult to remember to drive on the other side of the road? How about sticking a reminder note on the steering wheel every time you get out of the car?
- Never rely on the advice of a front-seat passenger when overtaking… assess all situations yourself, by easing the car out gently until you have a clear view.
- Know the speed limits in each country you drive in.
- French police calculate your speed using the time and distance you drive between Péage toll booths.
- Foreign police are strict on drivers obeying STOP signs.
- If stopped, be as calm and polite as possible, this is a no-win situation and getting irate will only inflame the situation.
- On the continent you must

Driving cultures vary hugely around the world… but if you can survive New York, you'll survive almost anywhere

always carry a red warning triangle in your car and use it whenever necessary.
- A First Aid kit and spare light bulbs should be carried in France. Other countries have other rules. Check before you go.
- A continuously flashing amber light at traffic lights means you can continue with care but should be

prepared to give way.
- Never over-estimate your distance targets each day. Plan for a safe and leisurely drive and always avoid driving when feeling tired.
- Buy a good road atlas and plan your route carefully.
- Carry copies of your vehicle documentation with you at all times, and include a European Accident Report Form.

In America, hire car insurance can cost more than the actual car hire itself. It's best to deal with the major hire companies. This also guarantees you'll get a safe, new car.

Sweden changed from driving on the left to driving on the right at 5am on Sunday 3rd September 1967, that was despite the fact that over 82.9% of the population voted against the change in a referendum.

The world's most dangerous road (outside of a war zone) goes from La Paz to Coroico in Bolivia which drops over 11,000 feet in 64 kilometres. Rain, mud, fog and 3000-foot drops mean it's one road probably best avoided.

World driver

If you are going to drive abroad, particularly in a strange country, try researching their driving habits and systems on the web before you go.

66 percent of the world's population drives on the right-hand side of the road, that's 3.84 billion people (in 166 countries). The other 1.93 billion people (in 74 countries), drive on the left-hand side.

We started driving (riding) on the left back in violent feudal times. Swordsmen buckled their sword sheaths to their left-hand side (as, like now, they were mainly right-handed). Therefore, to prevent passers-by being hit by their scabbards they'd ride on the left. Also, right-handed people find it easier to mount a horse from the left – but this would be impossible wearing a sword on your right.

Britain's most dangerous road is the A889 between the A86 and the A9 near Dalwhinnie in the Scottish Highlands.

In France, if you can't pay your on-the-spot speeding fine, the police may impound your car. Most will demand cash rather than a credit card. The Gendarmerie will even drive you to the nearest cashpoint!

In India sacred cows get right of way. Drivers have been killed for running into a cow!

It can take up to seven hours to drive across Tokyo! Sometimes public transport is essential!

In Australia's Northern Territory you can drive almost 200 miles between petrol stations.

Never argue with trams! They cannot steer around you, usually have priority and are much bigger and heavier than you. Look out for tramlines, in European cities.

In Indonesia it's not uncommon to see someone carrying a carrier bag full of petrol to their car or motorcycle!

EUROPE

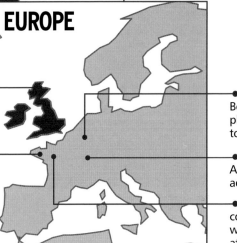

Cyclists have greater priority in countries like Holland, Belgium and Denmark than they do in the UK. Give them plenty of space, treat them considerately and be prepared to give way.

Despite the myths that circulate, very few German Autobahns allow unlimited speeding any more. Most adhere to the national speed limit.

When driving in France (and several other European countries) it is obligatory to carry spare lightbulbs, a warning triangle and a First Aid kit. You should also attach a GB or EU sign to your car.

Advanced towing

Pulling a caravan or trailer behind your car has associated dangers. Minimise them with IAM training

TOWING

If you tow a caravan or trailer, the IAM offers a towing test in partnership with the Camping and Caravanning Club.

IAM TOWING TEST
The towing test is specifically geared towards raising standards of safety and enjoyment when towing or manoeuvring a caravan or trailer.
Not only is it directed at those members enjoying the freedom of caravanning, but also, horsebox, light commercial and casual trailer use.

Preparation for the test is based purely around the IAM Advanced Driver scheme, with the addition of specific trailer maneouvring skills and techniques adding complexity to the drive.

TOWING TEST REQUIREMENTS
• A road legal vehicle with insurance and MOT
• Full driving licence
• Camping and Caravanning Club membership certificate
• A road-legal trailer

TAKING THE TOWING TEST
The IAM have a discounted

agreement with the Camping and Caravanning Club (CCC), and it is a pre-requisite of the test that the CCC manoeuvring course is completed prior to booking an IAM test. This ensures uniformity in knowledge and training prior to any road driving.
The IAM towing test can be taken at a number of venues throughout the UK during the course of each year. For specific times and locations, log onto: www.campingand caravanningclub.co.uk. For more towing information check out: www.ntta.co.uk

ADVANCED TOWING TECHNIQUES

- Check the tread and pressure of the tyres on your caravan or trailer before every journey.
- To increase stability and control, keep the nose weight of the caravan or trailer high (25-75kg).
- Check your tow bar, brakes and light connections before every journey.
- Make sure any load is correctly secured and don't carry any pets or people in your caravan.
- Allow for the extra width of a trailer/caravan.
- Buy a set of extra-wide wing mirrors.
- Drive more slowly when towing, but be courteous to other road users by pulling over regularly to let them pass.
- Allow extra space when negotiating tight bends and corners.
- Increase your braking distances to allow for the extra weight. Brake gently to avoid jack-knifing. Think 'caravan' constantly, and drive accordingly.
- Unstable trailers and caravans can start to 'swing' from side to side in a pendulum motion at speed. If this happens, slow down gradually and consider adding more nose weight to cure the problem.
- For information and tips on manoeuvring your caravan or trailer check out www.campingandcaravanningclub.co.uk, write to Membership Department, Greenfields House, Westwood Way, Coventry CV4 8JH or telephone 0845 130 7632.

ADVANCED CHECKLIST
- Modify your driving line to take account of the size of your trailer or caravan.
- Always allow greater stopping distances.
- Make sure you understand the law regarding towing.
- Pull over regularly to avoid delaying other traffic.

EXAMINER CHECKLIST
- Is the entire drive carried out to IAM Advanced Driver standards?
- Are the speed limits of the vehicle and trailer/caravan taken into account?
- Does the driver recognise the challenges in positioning their trailer or caravan according to its size?

OTHER IAM PRODUCTS AND SERVICES

Driving Abroad
An excellent 224-page paperback guide by Robert Davies.
Ideal for anyone planning to drive overseas.

Driving Assessment
Keep your driving skills in tip-top condition with regular assessments
every two or three years.

Special Assessment
Take your driving up a gear with this excellent high-level
driving check-up.

Learn to be an Observer
Join the volunteer ranks of the IAM and help others perfect their
motoring techniques.

Senior Observer
Take your motoring skills to the next level and see how good you really
could be behind the wheel.

How to be a better driver

Notes

Notes

Notes

How to be a better driver

Advanced Driving index

www.iam.org.uk

After passing the Advanced Driving challenge

As an IAM Advanced Driver you should always drive in a way that sets an excellent example to other motorists. What's the point in training to be one of the best drivers on the road, and then not emphasising the point every time you get behind the wheel?
As an Advanced Driver, you have the skills to drive safely and progressively at all times, but IAM drivers never stop learning and should always seek to improve their driving.
As an IAM member you can continue to enjoy further challenges by taking a driving assessment or a more stringent test, known as the Special Assessment. Alternatively, consider retaking your test every few years to keep your driving skills honed to perfection.

Help others to become Advanced Drivers
Ask any 100 drivers how good they are and over 90 of them will tell you that they are above average. This is, of course, a mathematical impossibility – they are fooling themselves!
 If you really want to make the best use of your excellent, newly-acquired driving skills, the way forward is to consider helping others to become Advanced Drivers. You can achieve this worthwhile goal by joining the IAM group network as an observer. The IAM is always looking for new volunteers and observers to help deliver its national Advanced Driving agenda.

IAM Contact Details
IAM, IAM House, 510 Chiswick High Road, London. W4 5RG

Tel: 0208 996 9600
E-Mail: enquiries@iam.org.uk
Web: www.iam.org.uk